FROM DUSK TO DAWN

FROM DUSK TO DAWN

Maggie Barrett

ISBN: 978-0-9966730-0-6

Interior design by Claudia Martinez
Jacket design by Joel Meyerowitz

For Isabel and Joel, with love

FROM DUSK TO DAWN

> PART I <

1

....

Tom raised his window shade hoping to find dawn out there in the great beyond, but all he saw was his reflection against the mid-Atlantic night. Seeing that same face he had stared at in the mirror as an adolescent, he wondered now, as he had then, why the symmetrical planes and even features fell shy of handsome.

He pulled down the shade and reclined in one of a pair of business class seats. The one next to him was unoccupied. This had been a relief when he first boarded, but now, instead of guaranteeing privacy, it added to his sense of separation. The seats across the aisle were also vacant and for an anxious moment, he wondered if he was flying alone, if he would forever be flying alone through the night. Even the flight crew had disappeared, having done their duty for the time being. Where did they go? It was always the same on these overnight flights from JFK to Heathrow; a moment always arrived, after the last cognac was poured and an extra pillow fetched, when they seemed to vanish into thin air. He was briefly amused by the image of the crew being sucked out of the cabin into the atmosphere. And then he winced as he heard the groan Lily would have made as she always did when she finally got one of his jokes.

He closed his eyes, even though he knew he wouldn't sleep. He never could on these flights. Lily used to tease him that it was because he was a control freak and needed to stay awake in case the pilot succumbed to narcolepsy. Was she asleep yet? He envisaged her readying for bed: the methodical way in which she removed what little make-up she wore; the tender massaging of cream into the skin of her face and neck, looking this way and that to make sure she didn't miss a spot. He was always fascinated by this nightly ritual and the way in which she managed to both reveal herself and yet stay hidden, as if the make-up was a subtle mask that hid a more complex one.

He opened his eyes again and checked his watch, which was still on New York time. It was eleven at night there, so that made it four in the morning in London. Another three hours before touchdown. But what time was it up here? He felt the loneliness of being neither here nor there.

He put his watch forward to Greenwich mean time and wished it were that easy to enter the future, to leave the past back there in another time zone.

He took the airline's magazine from the seat back and flipped through its pages, only to find, like everywhere one looked these days, more hype about the imminent arrival of the new millennium. Disgusted, he replaced it, and closing his eyes again listened to the drone of the engines, wondering how he'd make it through the next uninhabited hour before the plane came to life again, the crew magically reappearing with breakfast and freshly made-up faces beaming with professional cheer. How was it possible to fly through the night at thirty-five thousand feet in a metal tube and arrive at one's destination unscathed?

2

....

"You're like an old woman, you are," Jocelyn teased, as Charles checked his pockets once again for glasses, key, and wallet.

"Well, let's hope you're as gorgeous as I am when *you're* an old woman," he shot back with a grin. She started to roll her eyes, but softened as he kissed her. It was one of the big differences between them, this difference in tempo. Charles, was an *adagio*, while she was definitely *allegro*, and although she knew that when they were in concert it was a good thing, too often she found herself impatient with his unhurried approach to life. Then again, she thought, as he slowly withdrew his tongue from her mouth, when it came to lovemaking he could take all the time he wanted.

They were on their annual trip from New York to England. Most years, they would spend a few days in London soaking up theatre and museums and revisiting Jocelyn's favourite haunts before dutifully heading down to Cornwall to meet Jocelyn's brother and sister-in-law. Being on neutral ground, they usually managed to bring their four disparate personalities and life-styles into some sort of civil arrangement. At least they could all enjoy the scenery while pretending to ignore their judgments of one another.

Kenneth and Sarah were already waiting in the lobby of the hotel. A pseudo-modern eyesore on the harbour front, the hotel had been Kenneth's choice this year in contrast to the quaint inn at the top of the village which Jocelyn had chosen last year and to which the four of them were now going for dinner.

Jocelyn adored her brother. He was the one constant in her life and though they were fifteen years apart and had virtually nothing in common besides some physical traits, there was an unspoken bond between them. Was it simply that he had always been her big brother? Her sister-in-law, Sarah, she felt no bond with. Never had and didn't really care. Well, that wasn't quite true. She actually cared a great deal that her brother had settled for so little in life. Not that Sarah was a bad person, just a bit bland . . . until you put a drink in front of her and then she could be downright embarrassing.

"You look lovely," she said, giving Sarah a kiss on the cheek, both of them knowing that the first lie of the evening had just been uttered. The petite prettiness that had been Sarah at twenty-five now carried an extra twenty-five pounds. She wore a black pleated skirt and blue lambs-wool sweater, chosen, Jocelyn was sure, to bring out the blue in her eyes. And she couldn't help but notice the Barbour jacket Sarah had been wearing for the last ten years, slung over her arm. Kenneth, who had retained his six feet of spare frame, gave a youthful impression until one noticed the gaunt lines in his face.

Unlike Kenneth, whose dirty blond hair had turned silver, Jocelyn's short crop had retained its coppery hue. She, too, had kept her youthful figure, but whereas Kenneth's energy was tightly contained by years of pinned-backed shoulders, courtesy of forty years in the British Army, Jocelyn's physicality had the restless sensuality of a dancer. She linked arms with him, looking fondly up at his careworn face as she gave him a squeeze. Perhaps he would relax a little as the evening progressed.

"Shall we walk up?" Kenneth asked, patting her arm. "Bit of fresh air before dinner?"

"Oh, I'm sorry," Charles said, "I should have asked. I ordered a cab . . ."

"Lord, how very New York of you," Kenneth said, giving Charles the once over. "Don't know how you stay so trim."

Kenneth noted the expression of relief that passed over Sarah's face. They had done the steep climb from the harbour to the top of the village last year; a fifteen-minute hike that had left her breathless and feeling inferior because the others seemed hardly to notice it.

A horn tooted out in the street, signaling the taxi's arrival. There was an awkward moment as they tried to figure out who should sit in the front until Charles opened the door on the wrong side and nearly sat on the driver's lap, a ruse that didn't fool Jocelyn. Charles was a surgeon, he never made left/right mistakes, but it was typical of him to try to help people relax and he had a mime's ability for the pratfall.

The weather had been iffy all day, but now, as the clouds scarred the moon and the first drops of rain splatted the windscreen, there was no doubt as to the season. Mid-November. If ever there were a country made for November, England would be it, Charles thought. The dreary, penultimate month that offered the natives the chance to practice their British cheer. The perfect month for a fallen empire, its dank weather carrying the ghosts of wars and ended love affairs. That this was the last November of the millennium only added to its forlorn quality.

Charles turned to the three Brits in the back seat, "So, do you think," he asked, "that the damp is responsible for your famous dry wit?"

Kenneth and Sarah chuckled, but Jocelyn, for whom comparisons between England and America often served as a point of contention between her and Charles, parried, "No more than America's *lack* of wit bears any relation to its surplus of wealth."

"*Touché,* baby!" Charles knew Jocelyn well enough to respond to her parry with a climb down.

By the time they reached the top of the village the rain was heavy, and as they turned onto the lane and the lights of civilization disappeared behind them, the headlights only served to illuminate their isolation. The driver slowed to cross the narrow bridge before bumping them over the rutted driveway to The Morvah, whose ivy-covered, stone walls and lit windows were reminiscent of a bygone era.

They pulled up close to the door. Charles refusing Kenneth's offer, paid the driver and the four of them dashed inside.

"Come in, come in," the proprietor called out, coming from behind the reception desk to shake their hands. "Good to see you again," he said, relieving the women of their coats. " 'Fraid it's rather quiet tonight. Bit slow this time of year. Will you come into the bar for an aperitif?"

"That would be nice," Sarah said, and Jocelyn and Charles exchanged the briefest of glances.

Jocelyn sat on the banquette as the others stood at the bar ordering their various potions. It amazed her that even though she no longer felt the urge, never mind the need, to drink, she could still look at every bottle on the shelf and instantly remember the taste of each one's contents. Charles, never a drinker himself, was happy to share a mineral water with her. By the time the proprietor had uncorked a bottle of Chardonnay and poured a glass for Kenneth, Sarah was already half way through the martini she'd ordered and asking for a top up.

"Come on, darling," Kenneth managed a tight-lipped smile, and took Sarah's arm. "Let's go in and sit down." Already visibly anxious, he guided her to a table and pushed a basket of bread towards her. "Have a bit of this," he urged and when she ignored him he tried to make light of it. "Oh go on, it's granary, your favourite." She complied, but not before taking another sip of her drink.

The dining room was empty, a hushed ruby interior all dressed up with nowhere to go. The rain, now torrential, was running down the windows as if to flee the wind, while violent gusts bullied the rhododendrons into scratching at the panes in a futile attempt to gain entry.

"Let's take this table," Jocelyn said, pointing to one in the middle of the room. "This way we can be the centre of no attention."

"Yes, why not." Kenneth scraped back his chair, helping Sarah to her feet.

"The waitress will be right with you," the proprietor said. "If you've got everything you need, I'll bid you bon appetite. She'll look after you."

Somewhere nearby a clock struck eight and as the last chime pealed, a young man, rather good-looking Jocelyn thought, entered the room, paused for a moment and with a brief nod to the foursome, made his way to the far corner of the room. As he passed, Jocelyn noted the designer jeans, black cashmere turtleneck and the expensive loafers. His short, almost black hair and blue eyes were a combination that Jocelyn had always found attractive.

How interesting it was, she thought, that one person could change the atmosphere in a room. With this man's entrance, her table had gone from chatty if somewhat forced conversation, to a silence interrupted only by Sarah's whispered request for the bread basket. It was as if this stranger had the ability to make them suddenly conscious of their discomfort with one another; everyone except Charles, whose quiet confidence was often misinterpreted by Kenneth and Sarah as American brashness.

"Where's that waitress?" he said. "I'm starving." As if on cue, a young woman bounced into the room, her face flush with innocence beneath a ponytail of titian curls, her short black skirt and tucked-in white blouse immediately identifying her as the waitress, while her Doc Marten lace-ups belied a bit of dated punk.

"Good evening one and all," she said in a cheery Cornish drawl.

Tom Ashton looked up from his book and immediately his eyes locked onto her, following her across the room. Caught slightly unawares by the girl's attractiveness, Kenneth shoved a piece of bread in his mouth and smoothed the napkin on his lap.

"Aha, and here she is just like the genie out of the lamp," Charles quipped. "And a very good evening to you too."

"So, who's going first?" asked the waitress.

3

....

When Tom had arrived at Heathrow earlier that day he'd taken a taxi to his flat in Primrose Hill. As he turned onto The Crescent, he felt overwhelmed by loneliness. The thought of seeing Lily's toothbrush in the bathroom was an image of intimacy that felt unbearable to him, in spite of the fact that it was the only thing she ever left there. On an impulse he asked the driver to take him to Paddington Station instead, where he searched the departure board for the earliest train to an unfamiliar destination. A ten o'clock to Penzance was flashing its boarding sign. With five minutes to spare he dashed to the ticket window, bought an open return, raced to the platform and settled in his seat just as the train pulled out. Cornwall, off-season. How perfect he thought; cheap, cold and deserted.

He had no idea where he would go on arrival and didn't much care. He'd slept most of the way down, arriving late afternoon, the dark of November already descending. The taxi driver, upon hearing Tom's request for somewhere to stay far away from it all, suggested The Morvah. Half an hour later, the proprietor, whose pale exterior was enhanced by the inn's ruddy interior, was proudly showing Tom upstairs to the master suite, remarking on how fortunate Tom was to be the only overnight guest as this was the room of choice. The suite overlooked the sea, which, although barely discernable in the dark, could certainly be heard as it crashed on the rocks at the foot of the cliff. Tom noted the four-poster bed and let irony trump grief. Lily loved four-posters.

After a shower and change of clothes he'd gone downstairs for dinner, the grandfather clock in reception heralding his arrival, which, again, he'd found ironic as he assumed he would be dining alone. So it was a bit of a shock to find a table, centre-stage, occupied by two couples. He'd paused, feeling the effrontery of it, and for a brief moment considered retreating to his room, but having eaten nothing for more than twelve hours, he let hunger guide him to a table in the far corner, far enough away to not be privy to their conversation but close enough to observe the nature of their group.

The waitress, undoubtedly striking, had taken his order and now brought over his single-malt whisky. He took a sip and turned his attention back to his book. But before long he felt himself being watched and looking up again, saw that the younger of the two women was gazing at him unflinchingly. She was attractive in the slightly dangerous way that women who have survived their own beauty tend to be. In her mid to late forties, he guessed, and yet ageless, partly because of the short, impish cut of her hair and partly because of the chiseled features, the erect bearing and the eyes that were both playful and challenging. A clever woman, he suspected, a woman who had, perhaps, gone beyond the pale more times that she should have and yet was still alive. She smiled at him and he gave a brief nod before returning to his book.

The waitress returned to take his food order. He asked for the pâté, relieving her, he assumed, of the pronunciation, followed by sirloin steak. "Excellent," she said, and walked over to the other table to take their orders. He found himself watching the woman again. His mother would have looked like her, he thought. If she'd still been alive, she would have been about the same age. His mother had been a mere seventeen when she had Tom, not quite twenty-five when she left him and his father, and dead on the eve of her thirtieth birthday—from alcohol and barbiturates.

Tom looked at the woman's tall glass and assumed again, that she was imbibing still water and not vodka. Her left hand, seductively twirling the glass, was unadorned by jewelry or manicure. Her right hand was resting, or not, in her companion's lap. He caught the end of her sentence, something about the four-poster bed upstairs, "We had a great time didn't we, Charles?"

The name issued from her like a soft wave on sand and Tom could hear his mother's voice calling to his father from the bedroom, all those years ago. "Charles, where are you?" Tom's father had been standing next to the stove, buttering her decrusted toast, the four-minute egg already in its porcelain cup, the Lapsang Souchong brewing in the Staffordshire teapot, his father's lips thinned by resentment, while the boy's porridge burned on the bottom of its neglected saucepan.

After a few minutes, the waitress returned with a huge tray balanced on her capable shoulder almost dropping a curtsey as she served Tom's pâté. "And the same for you, madam," she said as she walked to the other table, placing another pâté in front of Jocelyn, before serving Sarah and Kenneth shrimp cocktails, and snails for Charles, who, Tom was surprised to hear, spoke with an American accent. Tom had imagined he was European, something about his quiet elegance, the cut and fabric of his jacket and the way he sat, both regal and relaxed. He had the manner of one who knew his worth and understated it, thereby quietly increasing his value. No, Tom would never have taken him for an American; the woman, yes, but not him. Looking at the other man, Tom thought he might be the woman's brother, he had the same slant to his features, the same blue eyes and well-proportioned plane between cheek and chin, but where all her physiognomy came together in vibrancy his seemed to fall apart into resignation.

By now quite hungry, Tom dug in to the pâté enthusiastically, enjoying the rustic bread and the Cornish butter and finishing rather quickly. He noticed how efficiently the waitress cleared the tables, announcing that the main courses were being prepared by chef. Tom's steak arrived. Though generous in proportion it lacked tenderness. He did his best to wash it down with claret, but found he suddenly had no appetite and so retired to the lounge as the foursome awaited their desserts.

The lounge was comfortably chintzy with a sofa and four wingback chairs. A well-built fire was giving off a nice blaze of heat. Rust velvet curtains had been partially drawn leaving just enough of the gruesome night visible to make one glad to be inside. Tom helped himself to coffee and a cognac from the mahogany trolley and taking one of the wingbacks to the left of the fireplace, opened his book. He'd picked up a copy of Richard Ford's *Women with Men* at JFK and was glad to lose himself to the misery of someone else's affair.

From time to time, laughter drifted in from the dining room where the couples were no doubt stuffing themselves on trifle and clotted cream. The younger woman, he was sure, had a capacity for sweets, the intake of which would never be reflected in her weight, much like his mother, whose thin frame belied her hunger for sugar, while her surface sweetness hid a bitter heart. Women, he had long ago learned, were never what they appeared to be, in spite of their constant concern with appearance. Perhaps, he thought, this was their craft, the tool with which they protected their supposedly vulnerable position in life; a craft of self-awareness cultivated to such a degree that a woman could face any situation armed with what on the surface appeared to be disarming candour, but which in fact, was a carefully constructed demeanor.

"Would you mind if we joined you?" The woman stood in the doorway, the others dutifully behind her.

"Feel free," Tom said, looking up at her. She was, as he had guessed, of medium height, slim, the black jeans and boots just

shy of trendy. Both men were a head and shoulders taller, while
the other woman was, as they say, pleasantly plump and sensibly
dressed, her salt and pepper hair cut in a chin-length pageboy.

Charles and Jocelyn settled into the sofa opposite the fireplace
while Kenneth and Sarah took the two wingbacks to the right of
the fireplace so that the group was aligned somewhat like judge and
jury. Tom closed his book and awaited the inevitable inquisition.

"Are you on holiday?" Jocelyn asked.

"No," he replied, curious to see where she'd go from there.

She introduced herself, her brother and sister-in-law and her
companion.

"And this is my man, Charles," she said.

Tom looked at him to see how he felt about being referred
to as the butler, but Charles merely crossed one long leg over
the other, put an arm around her shoulder and waited for her to
continue.

"It's so hard these days to know how to describe one's *other*,
isn't it?" She went over to the trolley and poured cognacs for Kenneth and Sarah, a tea for Charles and coffee with two after-dinner
chocolates in the saucer for herself. "I mean, at our age 'boyfriend'
is a bit laughable, isn't it? I've tried 'companion' but it sounds too
much like someone who reads to the elderly. 'Lover,' of course,
would be perfect, except that it's been co-opted by the gays. So,
there you are."

And there *you* are, thought Tom, and looking at her could see
a slight crack in the surface through which disappointment could
be glimpsed.

The next few minutes passed harmlessly enough with the five
of them providing each other with the bare essentials of their
lives, such as from whence they hailed, and where they currently
resided.

"Oh, London," exclaimed Jocelyn, in response to Tom's answer. "You lucky thing. I spent a couple of years there in my teens

and it's still my favourite city. Charles and I live in New York. Charles was born and bred there, so ..." She let the sentence hang and ate her second chocolate.

Tom turned to Charles. "I spend quite bit of time in New York," he said. "And frankly I much prefer your city. I find the American attitude so much more refreshing."

Charles uncrossed his legs and removed his arm from Jocelyn's shoulder. "How do you mean?" he asked, leaning forward.

"Well," Tom said, "Americans are so willing to keep their eye on the future, aren't they?"

"Yes," Jocelyn interrupted. "But the future isn't everything, is it? The trouble with Americans is they're always throwing out the past the minute it happens."

"I should have thought you'd like that," Charles said, a slight edge in his voice. "You're the one who's always talking about letting go of the past."

She put her hand on Charles's knee and leaned forward, "You're terrible, you're always twisting my words, but you know what ... ?"

"Come on, darling. You're the greatest advocate for letting the past look after itself. I agree with Tom, the future's ..."

"Actually, what am I saying? The future's a joke," Tom interjected, his voice betraying more irritation than he'd expected.

"Maybe," Charles said. "But you know ..."

"Yeah, you know what?"

He reached into the inner breast pocket of his jacket and pulled out the small blue velvet box.

"Here's *you know what*," he said. "How's this for throwing out the past the minute it's happened!" With that, he hurled the little box across the room to Jocelyn who reached for it as automatically and eagerly as a young girl catching the bridal bouquet. Tom watched as she opened it, and heard her gasp as she saw the solitary diamond raised up in its platinum setting. She looked first to Charles and then to Tom, who saw in her eyes the desire that he had been so sure he would see in Lily's eyes barely forty-eight hours earlier. Lily, sitting across from him at the Four Seasons. Lily, who had looked at the ring and then at Tom and then closing the box had said, "You know what . . . ?"

4

....

Jocelyn knew, with the certainty of a Zen moment, not only what it was that was hurtling towards her but that she would catch it; that it would smack into her palm, that her fingers would close around it with all the excitement of rightful ownership and then, tenderly lifting the hinged lid as if releasing a butterfly, she knew that the Tiffany diamond set proud on its platinum throne not only wasn't hers, but that what it stood for was not within reach. And yet, as the room went silent, the diamond glittering cruelly in the firelight, she turned to Charles in anticipation and watched as the colour left his face.

That they would marry had, in the first months of their coming together, seemed not only a possibility but a certainty. He'd said as much. "When we get married I'm going to shout it from the rooftops," he'd declared, in response to the news that an ex of hers had recently married quietly. It seemed ridiculous now, that she would have believed Charles's declaration. Shouldn't the fact that her ex, whose need to be in the limelight at all times had been his contribution to the failure of their marriage, had married without fanfare, have been proof that one should never believe what men said? But she *had* believed Charles. His declaration had come out of him and towards her with all the force of the hurled engagement ring.

What had happened? She knew Charles loved her, and she him; knew that it would all stop with him; the years of search-

ing for love, years of drink and abandon, as if to abandon herself assured her of eventual rescue. Someone out there wanted
her, surely? Yet abandonment in some form or another was her
nametag, announcing her arrival into every room or relationship
she entered; the label that informed others as to how they should
treat her.

The dry, blue lips of the little box closed with a velvet whisper, although to Jocelyn it sounded more like a hiss. Perhaps, she
thought, it was the sound of venom; the spite of unrequited love,
and for a moment wished that she could be that cruel. Instead she
held Tom's gaze as she got up and walked over to him. She held
the box out, "I'm sorry," she said, and when he didn't reach for it
thought, for one mad moment, that she could keep it.

"What are you sorry about?" he said with a skeptical look.

"That things didn't turn out the way you had expected," she
said, gently placing the box on the arm of his chair. He turned
away from her.

"Well, it looks like they have for you."

"To some degree," she said, with the remnant of a smile.

The rain, which had been increasing steadily during the last
ten minutes, seemed to find a new reservoir, unleashing torrents
that slashed against the windows, along with gusting winds of near
gale force.

"My gosh," Jocelyn moved quickly towards the window, pulling the curtain aside. "It's cooking up a storm out there!" The
creaking and groaning of ancient trees surrounding the inn made
the whole scene seem like a corny crime novel from the '50s.
Jocelyn looked back into the room to see Sarah was visibly frightened, clinging to her brandy and to her husband like the crutches
they were.

As it happened, Sarah *was* frightened and didn't like the feeling, although these days she spent a great portion of her life in
that state. As much as the storm outside scared her, the disturbing

atmosphere of the lounge terrified her even more. Confrontation was not Sarah's forte.

"Kenneth," she whispered, "don't you think it best to leave before it gets any worse?"

"What, the weather or Anglo-American relations?" Charles asked in a brave attempt at humour.

"Oh Charles, don't be so mean," Jocelyn tried to make light of it but nonetheless, chose to stand by the fire rather than return to his side.

"Hang on," Kenneth interrupted, ever the pragmatic. "Sarah may have a point. It's hammering down out there. We may struggle to get a taxi to come out in this unless it eases up."

Like his wife, Kenneth also avoided confrontation unless it was between the covers of history books, particularly those about WWII; an interesting quality for a man who'd spent more than half his life in the army. Ever *prepared* to go to war he'd never actually gone to one. Along with the rest of his company, he had narrowly avoided the Suez Crisis; the Falklands War came and went without him and then he was too old. It hadn't been an illustrious career. As for the home front, he'd resorted to taking a frail leaf from his mother's book and retreated when things got complicated—especially in his marriage. Kenneth was a believer in Britain's wartime motto, "Keep Calm and Carry On." That his courage had never been tested had been his downfall.

"Shame to break up the party," Tom said with only a hint of sarcasm. He had originally assumed that the party of four were staying at the hotel, and had been relieved during the course of dinner to learn that they weren't and that he therefore wouldn't have to face them at breakfast. But now he felt a little disappointed that what was promising to be an interesting evening might soon be curtailed.

"I'm with you, Kenneth," Charles was strongly advising that a taxi be called immediately when the waitress came into the room to announce that the bridge, halfway down the lane, had been washed away, making their departure moot.

"We've called emergency services," she said, "but it's pretty unlikely it'll be sorted before morning." She looked around the room to gauge the reaction and then, seeing that the plump woman was on the verge of panic, added, "But look, it's OK. I can ring Trevor—that's the owner—and I'm sure we can organize some rooms for tonight—it doesn't look like there's any other option. He might even give you a discount!"

"A discount?" exclaimed Kenneth not getting the joke. "I would have thought the civil thing would be to just put us up. Well, never mind. We'll wait awhile and see what happens."

"Oh, don't worry, Kenneth," Jocelyn said. "We'll cover the cost, won't we Charles?"

"Absolutely."

"That's not the point," Kenneth blurted out. "I mean, thank you. But no, it's just that we're already paying for the hotel down in the village."

"Maybe we could stay, Kenneth. They may not even charge us since it's really out of our hands," Sarah said hopefully, declining to add that it would be the Christian thing to do.

"Well," said Jocelyn, "if it gets any worse we'll be abseiling down the cliff and walking two miles along a stony beach in the dark, possibly at high tide, so I don't think we have much choice . . ."

"You'll have us all drowned on the rocks in a minute," Kenneth said, trying to sound jolly. "But really, I'd be happy to wait it out on the couch, unless there's a charge for that, too?"

"Oh, no sir," she said. "You'd be quite welcome, I'm sure. But I will have to check with Trevor first."

Trevor had inherited the hotel twenty years earlier, but his heart had never really been in it. The building and land had been in his family for nearly three centuries. And in spite of his wife's pleas to update, the place had barely kept up with the twentieth century, never mind being prepared for the new millennium.

Tom's father had been a penny-pincher, too, except when it came to his wife. He had lavished her with gifts at Tom's expense. A cost that robbed him of a bigger Meccano set and, eventually, entrance to any of the top boarding schools. As a result, he had been determined never to let money get out of hand in his own life. More than that, he decided that money would *be* his life. To that end he had worked his way through an undergraduate business degree before moving onto a graduate degree in international corporate law and was well on his way to making money from other people's money, having concluded it was the only risk-free way of becoming wealthy. Tom was confident that he was well prepared for the new millennium.

He looked at the little blue box, still balanced on the arm of his chair and could imagine the diamond sitting smugly on its perch. He had the urge to fling it in the fire but money, having already become the main artery of his existence, dictated that he pocket it until he could return it to Tiffany's on his next trip to New York.

"What should I tell Trevor?" the waitress asked.

"We'd like to wait a while," Charles said. "Maybe the road crew will show up in a couple of hours. After all, it's only nine-thirty. What do you all think?" he asked, looking around the room.

"Jolly good plan," Kenneth agreed.

And before either of the women had a chance to respond, Charles turned to the waitress.

"Perhaps you could ask Trevor if he could possibly help us out if the road isn't fixed by, say, eleven. If it's not too great an inconvenience."

The waitress nodded and turned to leave.

"What's your name, by the way?" Tom asked.

"Karenza," she said, with what sounded like some pride, before adding almost apologetically, "but most people call me Kerry."

"Well, Karenza," said Tom. "I assume you're stuck here too, so why don't you join us for a drink?"

"Oh yeah, thanks! I just have to sort things out in the kitchen. The chef's already left so it's down to me, as usual. Oh, and I'll ring Trevor," she said with a slight grin. "They only live in the next village, but it may as well be Mars."

Tom watched as Karenza gave a last look around the lounge before making her exit. He was aware that by inviting her to join them he was possibly sticking his neck out but felt that his own disappointment with Lily more than justified his seeking temporary solace. Besides he had felt the need to balance the numbers; now instead of four to one it would be six–nil. He looked across to Jocelyn and thought he saw a faint trace of disappointment lingering at the corners of her mouth.

In fact, she was disappointed, not only with his behavior, but because once again she had tried to reach out to a man as he struggled with his vulnerability, just as she had with Charles, whose manhood had been severely dented when his ex-wife left him for a friend. He had become quite adept at retreating from pain, which Jocelyn was happy to remind him of on a fairly regular basis. The need to rescue and comfort Tom had risen in her the way it does in certain women who believe love conquers all. And once again she had failed.

Tom was perfectly aware of how it must look—she probably thought it a mercenary move inviting Karenza to join them, and sadly predictable. But he didn't care.

In the meantime, Sarah had poured herself another brandy while her husband searched the bookcase for a possible distraction, a new take on war perhaps. Charles was in retreat behind an ancient copy of the *New Yorker* magazine. Jocelyn went to the drinks trolley for a mineral water.

"Would you like something?" she asked, turning to Tom. "Or have you already placed your order?"

The dig was not lost on Tom who sidestepped it without missing a beat. "I just thought as we're going to be stuck here for a while we may as well round out the numbers."

"But you have a room here, don't you?"

"Meaning?"

"Well, you could as easily have rounded out the numbers by subtracting yourself."

"But that would leave Karenza," said Tom, deftly returning the volley.

Jocelyn had years of practice at this game, and even though she hadn't played it for a quite a while she found she still had a good backhand.

"Like I said, you have a room here."

Having explained the situation to Trevor, who'd seemed more than happy to leave it to Karenza to sort, she gave the kitchen a quick tidy up before going to the small staff room where she kept her clothes. She changed into a pair of skinny blue jeans, tucking them into stiletto-heeled boots that laced up to the knee. They were this winter's splurge bought on a recent trip to Plymouth. As she tied the laces she mused on the scene in the lounge. She was well aware how she appeared to those people. She'd been working at the hotel since grammar school and had learned quickly that tourists like what they thought of as "some local colour," and tipped it well.

She rubbed her forefinger across the tip of a scarlet lipstick and then pressed the colour onto her lips until the stain was deep, its shade vying with the pale ginger of her hair. She left her heavy sweater in the cupboard choosing to wear only her black tee shirt, slightly torn at the low neckline and giving her shoulder-length curls a fluff made for the lounge.

5

....

Instead of returning to the couch, Jocelyn took her mineral water, curled up on the window seat and watched as the wind threw the rain against the panes. She wasn't afraid of storms, ever since her father had taken her outside during a thunderstorm when she was five. Never one for physical contact, her father had stood next to her on the back steps of the house marveling aloud each time the sky became a lavender expanse, awesomely illuminated with every flash of lightning. He had taught her how to count the seconds between a flash and the ensuing roll of thunder, each second measuring the distance between it and them; five seconds for every mile; the seconds diminishing until flash and thunder became a one-two beat and then, the point of danger having been reached, he'd taken her inside.

Over the years Jocelyn would learn to count the seconds between the flash in his eyes and the inevitable roar of judgment and anger that would ensue. The anger was only ever directed at her; never her mother or brother. The fact that he never actually became physically violent did nothing to remove the possibility.

As the Cornish sky let loose its own violence, Jocelyn remembered the tension between her and her father; how it had become so unbearable that she eventually provoked him into hitting her and, using that as an excuse, had left home the next month, barely sixteen years old.

She looked now at her brother, still standing at the bookcase;

her beautiful, buttoned-up brother. And then she turned to look at Charles who was completely absorbed by the article he was reading. Jocelyn thought about the men who'd come and gone in her life and it seemed to her that they fell into two categories of before and after: before getting sober she'd gone for the abusers, attracted by their physicality and the excitement of the flash. And then, as her drinking deepened along with her sense of worthlessness, she'd provoke them until they lashed out at her, always escaping serious injury, but each time having the justifiable reason for running away.

Now that she was sober she'd chosen a man who didn't have a shred of violence in him, but whose weapon of retreat matched that of her brother. She looked again at her brother, saw the pinch of the once full lips, the downward pull at the corner of his mouth and wondered now whether it *had* been the search for his courage that had attracted him to the army, or rather the need for a righteous place to channel the violence he feared he may have inherited?

Charles turned a page of the magazine and continued reading. She looked at his profile and felt the same warm surge of adoration she'd felt the first time she'd seen him, also in profile, as he'd studied an x-ray of her right breast. She'd gone to him for a second opinion. The first oncologist had insisted that because of where the area of concern was located and because she was so thin, she would require a surgical biopsy; a procedure which would remove an area of her breast somewhat akin to pitting a cherry as well as leaving a one-and-a-half-inch scar on the underside of her breast.

She had been nearly four years sober at the time and was just beginning to learn that decisions made in desperation tended to end in regret. And so it was that she had made her way to Dr. Charles Morgan, the highly recommended oncologist specializing in breast cancer at New York Hospital. An assistant had shown her into his office and she had been struck not only by the beauty of his profile and the silver curls that seemed to hold the energy of the wind behind his becalmed features, but also by the combination of gentleness and strength in those features. But it wasn't just his physical attractiveness that had sent that warm surge through her; it was the look of concentration that held both curiosity and caring, as if in looking at the black-and-white image of her breast he was captured by an entire universe. Such was the level of his concentration that it was a full minute before he became aware of her presence; at which point, when he turned to her, the shock of seeing each other had rendered them both speechless.

It was this quality that endeared him to her still, three and a half years later; his ability to remain oblivious to her presence, sometimes to the point where she found herself counting seconds to the mile, but always eventually turning to her as if seeing her for the first time, his pleasure in doing so spreading across his face the way a sunny morning dissolves the dark of night.

Another distant roll of thunder brought her attention back to the window and she watched again as the rain came in gusts; now an obliterating stream upon the dark glass, now relenting to reveal the shadows of the garden; the rhododendron knocking and scratching against the glass like a scared and hungry beast.

Charles was trying to concentrate on *The New Yorker,* but found his mind wandering to the recent events in the lounge. He hadn't really been paying attention when the ring arced its way across the room. He'd been distracted, discomfited in fact, by Jocelyn's comment about an appropriate way to introduce him. What was wrong with "boyfriend"? Was it really that laughable to be in one's fifties and be introduced as such? He agreed with Jocelyn that "companion" and "partner" were inappropriate, but why did anyone have to have a label at all? And he was, if he could actually allow himself to get to the feeling, a tad pissed off with her comments about America versus England. It was a point of contention between them that, because it so often arose whenever the subject of their relationship came up, he took it as a veiled threat; that one day, if he didn't marry her, she'd simply leave and return to England.

Why couldn't she just be happy with the way things were? Why, at their age, with no prospect of progeny, was there any need for marriage? Why did love never seem to be enough? And he did love her. He had from that first moment. He'd been surprised that he was still capable of such deep feeling after the defeat of his marriage. And why hadn't his ex-wife loved him? Had he really loved her? Or had he just been determined to "make it work" because in his work he could rarely make things come right? Sometimes, looking back, he thought his marriage had been a form of cancer; a malignant something at the core that kept on growing no matter how he tried to cure it. First with a puppy, later with a son and a brownstone on West 71st Street near the park, and in between the capitulation; the switch from psychiatry to oncology because, as Melanie had said, if he must choose a career in medicine he may as well choose the higher paying one. After all, she pointed out one night after having magnificently sucked him off, there wasn't much difference between a sick mind and a diseased breast; both required constant monitoring, the chance of a cure slim, remission unlikely and recurrence probable.

It occurred to him now, as he turned a page hoping to re-engage with the article, that he had been in a state of shocked confusion. It had both paralyzed his courage to move on as well as served as a retreat from the exploration of his own responsibility for the failure of his marriage. Certainly, his ex-wife had had an incurably sick mind, while Jocelyn still had, no small thanks to him, two beautiful, cancer-free breasts. Perhaps he'd chosen the right career after all. And, in spite of Jocelyn's fiery nature and, at times, the unbridgeable gap between their individual needs, he felt he had chosen the right woman. Yet in that moment when the little velvet box had landed with a thwack in the palm of Jocelyn's hand and she had opened it and turned to him, he had felt . . . what had he felt? Not exactly terror, more like a paralysis, maybe even impotence. A feeling that on some deeper level he would never be able to give Jocelyn what she wanted. But really, wasn't that bullshit? What did he think she wanted that he couldn't give? Fidelity? He had no doubt he could give that. As much as he loved women he'd never been a womanizer. He certainly could provide financially, and besides, Jocelyn was neither materialistic nor dependent. Unlike his ex, who'd never had to work and had spent her free time spending money, Jocelyn was a hardworking artist and a dedicated parttime professor at the School of Visual Arts. So what was his problem? Why not get married? It was the sickness and health thing; the "until death do us part." Even the great Dr. Morgan couldn't cure that.

A puff of perfume entered the room as Karenza opened the door, poked her head around it and looking at the glum group chortled, "Crikey, did someone die?"

There was a barely audible gasp from Sarah who, along with the others, had turned to Karenza. It took her a moment to figure out who this creature was who'd just entered the room. Then she realized it was the waitress. The girl she had been relieved to judge as beneath her. A ditzy local girl. Now she could see that the tables were somewhat turned, that once again she was the least attractive woman in the room, the least worthy of attention and she suddenly felt even more unsafe than she'd felt before from the combined threats of the storm and the provocative manner of the young man called Tom.

Before Karenza had returned, Sarah had been off in her own little brandy-hazed world. Thinking how she'd like to shop in the village tomorrow for some of that Cornish pottery she'd been collecting since the early days of her marriage. Its blue and white striped serviceability having then seemed representative of a life that would one day include an Aga and a Range Rover. She'd also been thinking, as she'd sipped her drink, trying to pace its inebriating glow so that she wouldn't be seen replenishing it for at least another twenty minutes; how it might be fun to get a room there for the night, to wake up to a full English breakfast and maybe go for a walk on the cliffs. And with the aid of the contents of her snifter she had imagined herself and Kenneth walking hand-in-hand, perhaps finding a grassy ledge to sit on and gaze out to sea before hiking on to the next village for a ploughman's lunch. But the sober truth was that she would still be asleep long after breakfast had been served. It would be Kenneth, alone, walking the cliffs, while she, struggling to regain some form of consciousness with the aid of a pot of strong tea and some dry toast, would do her best to look presentable for his return. It had long been their unspoken pact, and like all oft-repeated lies, had become something they both believed; that it was insomnia, not alcoholism from which she suffered.

For Sarah, waking up each day was akin to waking up from anesthesia; the dry mouth, nausea, disorientation, and the feeling that something awful and irreversible had happened. She awoke each day to the feeling that something essential had been taken from her, and that it had been taken from her because she was unfit.

The youngest of six children, the rest of whom had all gone on to have children of their own and, in some cases, grandchildren, Sarah had been the menopausal baby, growing up alone in a house with tired parents; parents who had already given what they had to five other children, from after-school classes to continental holidays and on to colleges and universities. By the time Sarah came along neither the will nor the funds were available. Her father, a once revered Episcopalian vicar, had quietly left his church after rumours of interference with choirboys, a rumour which both Sarah and her mother had refused to believe and which now her father had no memory of, having recently been placed in a nursing home and suffering from Alzheimer's. Sometimes Sarah wished she suffered from it too. After all, what in her life was worth remembering?

"Come on in," Tom said, leaping to his feet and offering his chair. "What would you like to drink?"

Karenza waited for another clap of thunder to cease and then, at ease in Tom's chair which now that she was in it took on the air of a throne, looked up at him, "A single malt, neat, please." She looked over at Jocelyn with a faint edge of triumph. Jocelyn got up from the window seat and returned to sit next to Charles. Holding the girl's gaze she said, "Great boots."

As Tom crossed the room with the single malt, looking appreciatively at Karenza's somewhat provocative outfit, he noticed Charles putting a protective arm around Jocelyn. Now that Karenza had joined them, there was a tangible regrouping. Kenneth, as he turned from the bookcase and saw her, flushed and slightly flustered, sat back down in his armchair, the book on Cornish tin mining carefully arranged in his lap. He didn't seem to have noticed Sarah replenishing her glass.

Tom handed Karenza her whisky and, having been unseated, took the remaining wingback to the right of the fire. The storm, now into its second hour and showing no sign of abating, had become a sort of outsider, taken for granted, almost ignored. Kenneth, having apparently recovered his equilibrium, got up to put more wood on the fire before returning to his chair.

"So," said Karenza, interrupting the somewhat strained silence, "what now?"

"Maybe there's something on TV," Sarah posited.

"There may be," said Karenza. "But it won't do us any good. The antenna got knocked out half an hour ago."

"Are there any DVDs?" Kenneth asked.

"*Fawlty Towers*, that would be fun," Sarah said. To which Karenza snorted, "We don't need to watch it, we're in an episode of it!"

Sarah, beginning to feel the courage of the brandy increasing along with her dislike of this girl, pushed on, "Well, perhaps we could play a board game, then."

"Good luck there," Karenza said. "You have a choice between Scrabble, which is missing half its letters, or Snakes and Ladders—the most boring game in the world."

"Why don't we invent a game?" Jocelyn offered.

"Like what?" Tom asked, suddenly interested. "Spin the poker?"

Kenneth glanced at Sarah's glass furtively—at the rate she was going they could soon play the original game with the empty brandy bottle.

Unfazed, Jocelyn continued, "Come on, we ought to be able to come up with something. We don't know how many hours we're going have to kill, after all." She looked around the room for inspiration. Noticing the regular sound of the clock ticking on the mantelpiece, she had an idea.

"How about something to do with the new millennium, since it's almost here?"

"But how can you can have a game about the future?" Kenneth asked somewhat defensively. "After all, none of us knows what it will bring."

"Oh lighten up, Ken love," Jocelyn teased. "Surely all of us here have hopes and dreams about it?"

"Well," Karenza interjected, "if you believe everything they're saying about Y2K, the dreaded millennium bug and all that, you can kiss goodbye to your dreams for a while. You'll be lucky if there's enough food to eat."

"None of that's going to happen," Tom said. "It's just another scam to frighten people."

"God, what a load of doom merchants!" exclaimed Jocelyn. "It feels like a landmark moment to me. A good time to think about what matters in life. Don't you think?"

"Absolutely," Charles added encouragingly.

"OK. So, how about this: We each have to think of the thing we most want for the year 2000. And then we take a vote to find out whose idea is the most popular."

"Cool," said Karenza, the flash in her eye suggesting that she saw the possibility for high drama.

"Oh, I don't think that's a good idea," said Sarah who, if the look on *her* face was anything to go by, was actually horrified by it. "I mean it is so personal . . ."

"Come on, Sarah," Jocelyn said. "It's just a bit of fun to pass the time and who knows, maybe we'll all learn something."

"OK," Tom said, sounding unimpressed. "But it's a bit flimsy. . . . Let's be a bit more specific. Instead of what we *want*, how about what we *believe* in and how that will impact on the future? So, we say the thing we most believe in and then justify it?"

"Oh, brilliant idea!" Jocelyn looked around the room eagerly to see if there was general accord.

"And the prize for the winner?" Tom asked, looking at Karenza.

"A free room for the night," she replied, looking right back at him.

"Good deal," he said. "I'm in. Anyone else?"

"Sure," said Charles, who already seemed confident.

Kenneth hesitantly raised his hand. "Why not?" he said.

"Wouldn't miss it for the world," Karenza said. Which left Sarah.

"Well, I'm not really sure about it, but all right," she said, as though she didn't have a choice.

Jocelyn had already found notepaper and pens in the desk and was handing them out.

"One word only," she instructed. "And when you're done, put your bit of paper in this," she said, reaching for a ceramic vase on the mantelpiece. "And then we'll pick them out at random. What fun!"

6

The lounge took on the studious air of an examination room; a question had been posed and to the likes of Tom and Charles, who felt very comfortable around ideas, there was only one winning answer and they each believed they had it. As they confidently scribbled, one resting on a book, the other on the arm of the chair, the others looked more circumspect. Sarah had already ripped up three scraps of paper, unsure how to proceed. If she were to write down the one thing she believed in she knew she'd be open to ridicule and so she opted for something more generic, believing it to be airtight. She folded her paper in half and in half again, mistakenly thinking, in her alcoholic stupor, that the authors of each belief would remain anonymous.

Kenneth felt stymied; he wanted to write at least a sentence and, as was often the case, felt annoyed that his sister, in spite of being younger than he, had once again made up the rules of the game. Karenza, knowing that her belief had a long way to go was nevertheless looking forward to arguing for it; believed fervently that without it, there was no hope for humanity.

Tom's belief lay in bold capitals upon the paper and, like Jocelyn's, was the only one to be placed in the vase unfolded. Kenneth, having finally settled on the word that best described his belief, was the last to place his paper in the vase, at which point Jocelyn took the vessel from the mantelpiece and placed her hand over the opening and gave it a good shake.

"Hang on a minute," Tom said. "So what happens now?"

"What do you mean?" Jocelyn asked.

"Well, for instance, who picks first and then what?"

"Oh, right, good point," Jocelyn said. "I suppose we could pick in alphabetical order, then whoever is chosen has to define their belief . . ."

"Then what . . . ?"

"Well . . ."

"Well obviously," said Charles, "then we argue the toss."

"Oh! But why do we have to do it like that? Why can't we just secretly vote on it, you know, ten being the highest?" The noticeable dread in Sarah's voice was rising along with the brandy consumption.

"No, Charles is right," Tom said. "You've got to be able to challenge a belief in order to discover whether it holds water or not. Besides if we go straight to a vote the game will be over in ten minutes, then what?"

"Back to Snakes and Ladders," Karenza said.

For Sarah this was way worse than Snakes and Ladders. She was sure that there were more of the former and maybe only one of the latter and that even that, with her luck, would be missing a few rungs.

"So," Jocelyn said, "the rules are set. Let the game begin. Charles, my darling, I do believe you are in the lead alphabetically." She held out the vase to him and watched as he extracted and unfolded the first scrappy-looking strip of paper.

7

....

"God," said Charles.

"What's the matter?" Jocelyn asked.

"Nothing," he replied. "*God* is the belief." He could have placed a bet on who had written this and found himself torn between derision and pity. He looked at the scrawl and wondered how on earth Sarah was going to defend it, especially as everyone, with the exception of Kenneth was already looking at her in disbelief. Out of politeness Charles asked whose it was, rather than asking who the hell believes in God.

"Mine," Sarah said, panic rising in her throat along with some acid reflux. Even in her muddled state, she could sense the cynicism in the room. How ironic, she thought. She should have stuck with her original choice. It was Jesus she believed in, had clung to. Not God. She hated God. You could serve God and still be cruel and unfeeling, and He didn't seemed to care. But Jesus had existed, was a healer—and there'd been many times when she needed the comfort of his words. She saw at once her folly but she was stuck now in a limbo of her own making.

"God?" exclaimed Tom. "Well, I can safely say I wasn't expecting that!"

"Now just a minute," Kenneth interjected firmly. "You could at least give Sarah the chance to justify her belief." He was sitting bolt upright now and tugged nervously at the lapels of his jacket as he crossed and uncrossed his legs. He shot Sarah a look, but made no further effort to come to his wife's rescue. He couldn't believe his wife was moronic enough to have put that in writing. It was bad enough he'd married a vicar's daughter, something that had caused him a fair amount of grief, his fellow soldiers having teased him mercilessly before his wedding night, telling him not to worry, that God was only the devil in disguise.

Jocelyn had never been close with her sister-in-law, but at this moment, as she saw her struggling and embarrassed, she felt genuine compassion for her. She had always felt that her brother had settled for the safe option when he'd married Sarah. She had been a docile girl in her mid-twenties back then, in complete contrast to the girl before her, a vivacious flirt who'd robbed Kenneth of his heart and all hope.

"So, Sarah," Jocelyn asked gently. "Why God?"

"Maybe the first question should be *which* God do you believe in," said Tom.

Sarah took another slug of brandy. "Well, there's only one God," she slurred.

"Um, really?" Karenza said. "I don't think Muslims and Jews and Hindus would go along with you on that one! I'm assuming yours is white, bearded and Christian?"

Sarah suddenly had a vision of her father, a "man of the cloth," in the pulpit in flowing robes and beard while hidden from view was a choirboy between his legs doing what God bade him do.

"As it happens," she said, "I am Christian but, you see I know everyone thinks that *their* God is the only God, it's just that well … I don't. They're all just different versions of the same thing … depending on what part of the world you come from."

"Well said, Sarah!" Kenneth seemed keen to wrap it up there before they got in any deeper and while Sarah was still reasonably lucid.

"And so you see God as the 'supreme creator'?" asked Tom.

"Of course, yes …"

"Creator of what?"

"Well, everything," she replied, as if surprised that this could be news to anyone.

"It's like being back at primary school," Karenza muttered under her breath to no one. "You really believe there's a god and what, you believe he created this whole sphere of chaos in seven days? Anyone need another drink?" She made her curvaceous way across the room to the drinks trolley. All eyes followed her either overtly or surreptitiously, Karenza slyly aware of the effect she was having. Kenneth was thinking it would have taken more than seven days just to make her. Tom was thinking he'd like to create havoc with her for seven hours. Charles was relieved he was no longer attracted to women like her, and Jocelyn wished her arse looked that good, while Sarah wished the God she didn't believe in would smite the damn woman.

Sarah knew all too well how foolish she must seem, but she hadn't anticipated, as she'd scribbled on that scrap of paper, how this barely considered idea would expose her. In fact, she'd worked very hard at ridding God from her life. As a girl, until she left home at eighteen for secretarial college, God had been the centerpiece of her home: grace before every meal, prayers before bed, Sunday school, church; her father muttering behind the closed door of his study from Wednesday morning until Saturday night as he toiled over yet another sermon. How many had he delivered over the thirty years he was vicar of their village church?

As a child, Sarah had watched with awe as her father climbed the steps to the pulpit every Sunday, the sermon tucked inside his bible that he held pressed to his chest. Yet Sarah had never once seen him refer to his notes. He would stand aloft, gazing down at his parishioners; and then it seemed, in those early years, he became God. For after all, God was everywhere, all the time; all-seeing, all-powerful and of course moved in mysterious ways as her father would remind his flock. It was the mystery that made it all right that this supposedly loving God could take as much as he gave. It was the mystery in which one must have faith; faith that He knew best when he gave the neighbours a Down's syndrome baby; faith that he knew best when he killed Sarah's aunt and uncle in a car accident and left their only child brain dead. And faith, even though tested, was not to be shriven during the nightly news of plagues and starvation, uprisings and torture, rape and murder. God had a plan. He knew best. It was not for us to question.

By the time Sarah was ten she knew the formula. It became a game to her to guess when and how her father would introduce his favourite theme: temptation. There were times she was tempted—to run screaming down the aisle—but the great warning of temptation always kept her pinned to her seat. How he loved to remind everyone of God's daily, sometimes hourly, test of our goodness and faith; temptation, the human defect that made us sinners from birth and to which we all succumbed.

Later, after the rumours began, Sarah wondered if it had been to himself that he cried out when he assured his flock that we all must fall but redemption could be ours if we only would repent.

At the age of thirteen Sarah had been sent to a Christian camp for two weeks, during which time she got her first period and surrendered to the temptation of having her breasts fondled. She also had won her first and only prize. One of the many competitions during those two weeks was for an original piano composition to accompany the Twenty-third Psalm: *The Lord is my shepherd. I shall not want.* It was the line, *He maketh me lie down in green pastures,* that had inspired her, having the evening before lain in the long grass of a meadow across the lane from the camp, where a fourteen-year-old boy with greasy hair had kissed and groped her, their wetness mingling with the evening dew.

Her prize had been a watercolour painting of Jesus walking down a lane much like the one next to the meadow. In the paint-

ing he was accompanied by children of different ethnic back-
grounds and it seemed to Sarah at the time that they were all in
deep conversation. The caption at the bottom of the painting read:
Jesus suffers the little children to come unto him, and she wondered
why it had taken her so long to find him. And she had cried, not
as the teachers had assumed with the joy of winning but from
relief; for if such a terrifying and unforgiving father as God could
have made such a gentle and loving son, then maybe there was
hope for her.

Having poured herself a generous measure of whisky, Karenza
sauntered back to her chair, and then looking at Sarah, said, "So
tell us, Sarah, do you also believe God created all men equal?"

"Yes . . . " Sarah replied, unsteadily.

"Then how do you account for the fact that some people go
through life without suffering while others suffer torture, rape,
racism, disease, whatever. What sort of God decides that shit?"

"Well that's not God doing those things is it?" Sarah said,
recovering slightly. "That's people doing that to each other."

"But people don't give each other cancer, do they?" Charles
said. "So if God creates everything what would you say his purpose is there?"

"Maybe it's a form of punishment for the way we live," Sarah
said, and knew as soon as the words were out that she was in
trouble.

"Isn't that a bit draconian?" Jocelyn bristled. "I mean, do you
really believe cancer is a form of punishment? How can you say
such a thing when your own mother died of cancer?"

"I say, Joss, that's extremely unfair," Kenneth interrupted.

"Oh, well, I'm used to that," Sarah said, draining her glass.
"After all, I believe Kerry over there, whatever her name is, asked
if God created all men equal. There was no mention of women.
And if you must know I think it was God's mercy my mother
died of cancer so she didn't have to live to see her husband lose
his mind and end up in a nursing home."

In fact, she believed her mother's cancer was indeed a punishment. A punishment for not having stood up for anything; for having churned out six children without emanating the least whiff of sexual appeal; for having stayed with a man who obviously preferred boys; for having told Sarah, when visiting her in hospital after the stillbirth, that Sarah was lucky to have had her uterus removed, that children were more of a burden than a blessing. Maybe it was that particular cruelty that made God punish her mother with ovarian cancer. God knew what he was doing.

"Well, if you don't mind me saying, I think God's a load of crap," Karenza said, swinging a booted leg in Sarah's direction. "I don't believe having more God in our lives will make things better in the millennium. It'd probably make things worse. I don't think your God or any other God exists. And I can't believe that anyone who calls themselves an adult can possibly believe in something so obviously absurd. That's just blind faith. In my book, believing in God is the ultimate excuse for not taking responsibility for your own life. And anyway, it's obviously a male invention. I mean, it's always a 'Him' isn't it? Allah, Buddha, Yahweh, whatever. Because men have to control everything, don't they? That's what God is; a manmade invention for controlling people through fear. And of course, man's biggest fear is women, right?"

"Oh, steady on," Kenneth laughed uncomfortably. "That's a bit rich isn't it?"

"You think?" said Karenza, looking right at him as she uncrossed her legs. "Why else put them upstairs at the temple, swelter them in a burka, cut off their genitalia, deny them abortions ..."

"All right, all right," Kenneth held up his hand. "We get the point."

"Does anyone else believe in God?" Charles chimed in. There was no response.

"Do you?" asked Tom.

"No."

"Why not?"

"Well, it's scientifically implausible, isn't it?"

"That may be true, but does science have the answer to everything?" Jocelyn parried.

"Most things, yes."

"But isn't that like saying science is God?"

"Jocelyn is shameless when it comes to twisting my words. You know very well, babe, I don't believe in any kind of God, religious or otherwise."

"Did you grow up with religion?" Tom asked.

"No."

"Really?"

"Really."

"Weren't your parents religious?"

"Up to a point."

Charles stood up abruptly, walked over to the fire, stoked it and threw on another log.

"Are you all right, darling? Would you like a cup of tea?" Jocelyn had moved over to him and stroked the nape of his neck. Charles looked at her gratefully.

"That would be wonderful," he said.

Tom pushed on, not sensing the subtle change in atmosphere. "So, what were they and at what point did they stop?" he asked.

Charles took the teacup from Jocelyn, and muttered a distracted thank you, before fixing Tom with a cold look. "The answer to the first question," he said, "would be Jewish. The answer to the second would be during the Holocaust." And then he sat down and stared into the fire.

Charles's parents had lost their parents, their daughter, cousins, aunts, and uncles in the Holocaust. In fact, his parents were all that had remained of their branch of the Morgenthau family. Through some miracle that had nothing to do with God, they had each managed to survive in separate death camps and after months of searching at the end of the war had found each other, emigrated to America, changed their name to Morgan and, in 1946, pregnant with Charles, embarked on what they hoped would be a new life in the new world. Whatever vestige of belief in God that remained was permanently eradicated in the spring of '47 when Charles's mother, still frail from years of malnourishment, had died in childbirth.

The fire came back to life, the flames already beginning to consume the new log. Charles sat before it thinking of all the fires, those hellish fires, fed with Jews; years of fires consuming the young, the old, the frail, the innocent, the cowards, the believers, the orphans, the lovers and the babies still in the womb. Fire without end.

"And you, Tom?" Charles said. "Do you believe in God? Your family?"

"No."

Tom took a mouthful of whisky and rinsed it over his teeth before swallowing. "My father grew up Episcopalian but has been lapsed ever since I can remember. My mother was an Irish Catholic."

"Was?" Jocelyn asked.

"Yes," Tom said, looking at what was left in his glass.

"What brought her to her senses?" Karenza asked, with a chuckle.

"Death. She OD'd when I was 13."

"Well, that would do it," Sarah mumbled.

"Jesus," Kenneth hissed, shifting in his seat, but unwilling to make eye contact with his wife.

Karenza turned to Tom, "How awful. So were you brought up with religion?"

"Oh yes. I got the Irish God courtesy of Mother," Tom looked down into his glass and knocked back the final dregs. "Evidently it was all she had to offer. My dad gave her everything she asked for, desperate to hold on to her. Even kowtowed to her God, and gave him to me every fucking Sunday until she died. Oh yes, I got the works; choirboy, confession, confirmation, the occasional feel-up from the priest, the caned arse by the headmaster, the shame, the fucking claustrophobia, you name it. If it weren't for the incense I might have OD'd myself."

The room went very quiet. The storm, unabated, suddenly sounded even louder by comparison. Charles got up and put his hand on Tom's shoulder for a brief moment before walking to the window to peer out. Jocelyn looked at him as he stood there, wishing she could console *him* with a pat on the shoulder but it seemed ludicrous in the face of all that he had lost.

Karenza went once again to the drinks trolley to refill both her and Tom's glasses and returning to sit by him asked, "What happened then?"

"What do you mean?" he asked.

"When your mother died, what happened to God?"

"I suppose she took him with her. Whatever remained of him, her bible and a rosary, my father threw on the bonfire in the back garden along with her wedding dress. He took me out of Catholic school and sent me to the local grammar."

But God hadn't been that easily removed from his life. Make-believe burns deep into the malleable brain of a child and until she'd died he had believed; he'd had no choice. After all, if his mother believed then there was hope that they would all be together again someday. Hope that she'd come back to him and his dad. And he'd been angry with his father for not believing; if he had, then maybe she wouldn't have felt so alone, maybe she wouldn't have died.

Unlike his father, who'd buried himself in serial affairs, Tom had set out for revenge, first by outing the priest, then by chalking a series of blasphemous statements on every blackboard in the school the day before his father removed him from it, and finally, by turning all his attention to study and advancement in the material world.

"So," he said, turning to Sarah, "how does my God compare to yours?"

Sarah felt trapped; he sounded exactly like hers, but she was too far in now. Only Jesus could save her. "Well, he certainly doesn't sound like the compassionate God I grew up with," she lied. Kenneth looked at her and wished she would just pass out. What was she doing? What was all this drivel about God? Was she some kind of born-again Christian for Gods' sake, and the Holy Spirit was booze? And then Kenneth made one of the few reckless moves in his life. Strictly a wine-with-dinner man and the occasional cold beer after a day of gardening, he walked over to the drinks trolley and poured himself a large gin.

"What about you?" Charles asked Karenza. "Where do you stand on God?"

"Right on his face in my Doc Martens," she said, and Jocelyn let out a hoot of laughter. "God was absent from our house, unless you count my father, who was an unrelenting bastard who called all the shots. No, that religious crap's not for me," she said, looking straight at Sarah. "Frankly, given Tom's and Charles's experiences I can't imagine how anyone in this room could still believe in God. But then, we haven't heard from Kenneth and Jocelyn yet, so maybe they can enlighten us?"

8

....

Kenneth was fifteen when Jocelyn was born and in the first years of her life, before he left home to join the army, he may as well have been God. Her big brother, whom she cried for every morning when he left for school, later for work, and beamed at when he returned. Her big brother, who brought ribbons for her hair, tickled her and made her laugh. Her big brother who bicycled home from school with an ice-cream cone for her and who, when she was five, had been the one designated to take her to church for the first time, depositing her on a wooden chair on the aisle while he disappeared to change into his choir robes. Jocelyn, an eager, curious child looking around the church, the stained glass windows lit up like Christmas, the flowers, the cross and that nice table with the fancy tablecloth, like the one their mother used for special occasions. She'd sat there, feet dangling, filled with excitement, sure that her brother had gone to fetch Santa Claus. But instead he came down the aisle carrying another big cross, choirboys and elders walking behind him. He'd winked at Jocelyn as he passed, and seeing she was about to exclaim had pursed his lips in a silent *shush*.

She was disappointed when Santa Claus finally appeared. Why was he wearing a white dress, and where had his snowy beard gone? And who was this God person he kept going on about? And when he declared that God is love, Jocelyn had sat on the edge of her chair and clapped her little hands, and the wooden chair folded up on her, threw her to the floor, and she ran down the aisle crying, "God doesn't love me, God doesn't love me." And that had been the end of church and God for her.

"So," Karenza asked, "who's going first?"

"Oh, age before beauty," Jocelyn laughed. "You go first Ken."

Kenneth, more than halfway through his gin, had passed through the stage where it had knifed him between the shoulder blades and was in the warm glow of inebriation where all is well with the world, and before the arrival of the nasties, as Jocelyn referred to the stage of drunkenness when one more is never enough and the one before has already ruined the good times.

"Well, unlike my *wife*," said Kenneth, looking at Sarah pointedly, "I can't say I actually believe in *God* although I do think there's something bigger than us."

"Like what?" asked Karenza, smirking. "T-Rex?"

Kenneth forced a chuckle, though his eyes betrayed that he was smarting slightly from the sarcasm. He took another mouthful of his gin.

Jocelyn, watching him in surprise, could see that his warm, tingly feeling was about to do a flip.

"Well, OK then," he said. He took a breath and sat up straighter, squaring his shoulders. "Frankly, I think the idea of God is ludicrous if you must know."

Sarah gasped and then frowned in confusion, but finding no words took another sip of her own drink. "Talk about hypocrisy," he continued. "All that talk about God is love and love thy neighbour. What a laugh. I mean look at war; most of them are caused by religion. And judgment, what about that? Where is the love there? Muslims hate Christians, Christians hate Jews, Episcopalians think their God is more elite than the Catholics' God. And talk about superstition. That men can be so brainwashed as to believe there will be virgins waiting for them when they pop their clogs, or that Saint Peter will be at the pearly gates checking to see if their name is on the list. Even the Buddhists, who seem harmless enough, are missing a sleeve. And what's with the rubbing your forehead on the ground and all the sweeties at the altar? I mean what a load of claptrap."

Sarah was looking at her husband as if she'd never seen him before. She hugged her glass to her chest as though it was the only available comfort she had as her already shaky world started to disintegrate beneath her feet. In her inebriated state, she couldn't figure out whether she was more stunned by his blatant betrayal or by his uncharacteristic forcefulness. Jocelyn, on the other hand, smiled appreciatively. She was thrilled and, although devoutly sober, tipped her cap at the gin in her brother's hand; it may be fool's courage but at least he'd located it.

"Mind you," Kenneth said, already beginning to feel he'd let something out of the bottle besides gin, "I do think one has to respect other people's beliefs."

"Why?" asked Tom, leaning back and folding his arms, almost by way of a challenge.

"Well, it's a small planet and there are a lot of us on it. If you don't want outright rebellion, sometimes it's better to keep your beliefs to yourself and let others believe whatever works for them."

"You mean like your believing that your mother gave birth to Jocelyn even though you never saw her pregnant?" The room fell silent. Sarah couldn't believe she had allowed these words to escape and felt, along with terror, a river of glee course through her.

"What are you talking about?" Jocelyn asked quietly, looking from Sarah to Kenneth. Having so recently acquired a little stature, Kenneth now suddenly seemed deflated, his shoulders slumping beneath his bowed head. As Jocelyn looked at him he reminded her of their father right before he had died. "I have no idea what she's talking about and obviously neither does she," Kenneth said, flatly. "Look at her, she's drunk." He gave his wife a look caught somewhere between hatred and sorrow.

Jocelyn, although so much younger than her brother, had felt protective of him since she was a teenager and once again stepped in to save him.

"It's OK, Ken. Anyway, I think it's my turn now," she said. "And then maybe we can give God a rest."

"No, but hang on a sec, Jocelyn. Are you just going to let her get away with that?" Karenza said. Having grown up in a family where there was daily drama she had a nose for the inherent drama in other families, perhaps even relished it. "What did you mean, Sarah? Why did you say that?"

Jocelyn stood up and took a step toward Karenza. "Look, why don't you just leave it? You're a vicious little girl, aren't you? Maybe before the evening is over we'll learn what made you that way."

Sarah, still feeling the glee and wanting to ride it, had just poured herself another brandy and began sipping it as she maneuvered her unsteady way back to her armchair, which seemed to have grown smaller, its arms squeezing the flesh of her hips. That was something else she resented about Jocelyn, and Kenneth, come to think about it. How come they could eat whatever they liked and still remain slim? Why, with all the drinking she'd done, did her sister-in-law still look gorgeous? And what right did Kenneth have, after all these years, to suddenly announce his disbelief in God? Why did she always have to be the odd one out? Hadn't she suffered enough? Who gave a shit about God? Evidently no one here, not even her. But whereas she had been defending a lie, she saw her husband's outburst as a betrayal. Why the sudden need to tell the truth, when it left her sitting there like an idiot? And suddenly, all the years of keeping quiet, of pretending her father was blameless, of keeping Jocelyn's secret, of pretending to believe in God instead of longing to be loved by Jesus, it all turned to bile. Her throat felt like a rust-lined wastepipe, the sewage backing up it. If she could no longer hold her own father accountable now that his mind had erased the tape, why should Kenneth and Jocelyn's father remain blameless?

"Because his mother *wasn't* pregnant with Jocelyn," she said. "Her sister was."

9

....

Jocelyn had been sixteen when she found out that her aunt was actually her mother. The enormity of the lie she'd grown up with was, when finally revealed, both a horror and a relief.

She was spending the night next door at her friend Pauline's house. The parents, who were teetotalers, had gone to bed early and Pauline, eager to taste the forbidden fruit, had dared Jocelyn to sneak home and bring back a bottle of something.

Jocelyn's mother was alone in the house; Kenneth by then long gone to the army and her father away on one of his solitary weekend hiking trips. The kitchen was dark when Jocelyn tiptoed in the back door. She'd assumed her mother was in bed reading and was retrieving a bottle of cooking sherry from the pantry when she heard her mother on the hall phone.

"I can't believe how bloody selfish you are, Jean!" Her mother's voice was charged with pent-up fury. "You've already abandoned her once. Australia, for God's sake!" Jocelyn had crept to the doorway to listen and stood there clutching the bottle as she heard her mother go on. "You hardly even know him, it's ridiculous! And what about me? You never think of me, do you. You fuck my husband, leave me to bring up the child. It's about time you took your responsibilities seriously. I brought her up as my own, Jean. And where have you been? You expect me to wish you bon voyage when you bugger off with some other waste of space? Forget it. He'll dump you the minute he realizes his mistake."

Jocelyn had stood there, fingers locked around the neck of the bottle, the bottle hugged to her chest as she took in what was being said. Then she had turned and quietly tiptoed out the door.

The lilacs were in bloom, their scent wafting on the night air, the air cool and damp and Jocelyn had crouched there beneath their shadowy branches and peed, the urine splashing her feet. A cat rushed by. A dog barked. One street over, a car braked suddenly, the tyres screaming as Jocelyn removed the cork from the bottle and took her first taste of alcohol before returning to Pauline's house. She'd said nothing of what had happened but insisted on listening to Jackie DeShannon's "What the World Needs Now is Love."

At dawn, drunk and dizzy, she'd crept out of Pauline's house back to her own. She'd barged into her mother's bedroom and shaking her awake had demanded the truth. She had watched without emotion as her mother wept and made Jocelyn promise not to tell Kenneth and then her mother had held her as she vomited all over the bed.

10

....

The look of agony on both Jocelyn's and Kenneth's faces made them look more like twins as opposed to the half-siblings they were now revealed to be. Jocelyn had feared this moment ever since she had blurted this piece of family business to Sarah towards the end of her drinking career. She and Sarah had been sitting together at Jocelyn's daughter's sixteenth birthday party. Mimi (later to be nicknamed MeMe by Charles's son, Jake) was already distant from Jocelyn, almost to the point of contempt and it was this that had turned Jocelyn's mood from proud if tipsy to sloshed and maudlin.

Jocelyn's date for the evening was sitting at the bar with Kenneth while she and Sarah remained alone at one of the round tables in the restaurant, most of the guests having already left. Jocelyn, feeling the need for intimacy, was sharing her regret at not having provided a sibling for Mimi.

"Perhaps," she had said, "Mimi and I would be closer if she'd had a brother or sister." Still willing, back then, to make excuses for her daughter's selfishness and judgmental behavior, Jocelyn had added that even though Kenneth was a lot older than her, and even though they weren't totally related, she would always be grateful for him.

"What d'you mean, 'not totally related'?" Sarah had slurred, well on her way to her own hangover. Maybe it was the drink or Mimi's imminent departure for boarding school or the knowledge that Jocelyn's date would only be just that; another one-night stand in the calendar of her life. Or maybe it was just one moment too many of loneliness and secrecy. Whatever it was, the words tumbled out. In that brief moment, Jocelyn held the misguided belief that because her sister-in-law had herself suffered so much loss, if she were to share the secret they would finally have something in common; it could be a source of comfort and compassion for each other. Yet underneath the need for connection and the even greater need to unload a burden, and in spite of her alcoholic haze, Jocelyn knew as the words left her mouth that she was possibly setting herself up for trouble somewhere out there in the misty future. But Sarah had sworn to keep the secret and because she had obviously meant it at the time, it had made it easier for Jocelyn to believe her.

Seeing her brother now, his face still pale, as he sank back in his armchair staring at the fire, Jocelyn was livid. She whipped round and confronted Sarah.

"How could you?" she hissed, glaring at Sarah. "You promised! And *you*," she said, turning to Karenza. "What makes you think you have the right to interfere in stuff that has nothing to do with you! The two of you are a disgrace."

The look on Karenza's face suggested she was appalled to find herself suddenly lumped in with Sarah, but she perhaps rightly judged this wasn't the moment to extricate herself. Sarah, unused to confrontation of this kind, felt more isolated than ever. The glee she'd so recently experienced now felt like a cinder block, the immovable weight of which rendered her mute and strangely devoid of feeling from the neck down.

Tom and Charles exchanged glances for a moment as if looking to find in the other, a way forward. The cruelty and tension in the room was unbearable but it was difficult to know who to confront or who to comfort. Charles knew his loyalty was to Jocelyn. At the same time, he found himself feeling resentful. How, in all the time that he and Jocelyn had been together, could she not have told him about this? And why, when they had from the beginning agreed to be honest with each other, could she have withheld such a thing? Wasn't it she who liked to quote the AA saying "You're only as sick as your secrets?" He felt hurt, slightly betrayed, and sad. He turned to reach for her just as she got up to go over to Kenneth. Kneeling beside him, she said softly, "Mum made me promise not to tell you."

Kenneth turned from the fire and stared at her.

"*What?*" he said. "How do you know about this? How could you possibly know?"

"I walked in on her. She was arguing with Jean on the phone. I didn't know what to do, Ken. I forced her to tell me, I was angry. Mum isn't my mum, Ken. Jean is." And as she told him she felt the absurdity of it magnify even as the burden eased. She felt numb really, as though it wasn't her story she was telling but that of a distant relative, handed down through the generations.

The room had grown chill. The fire needed another log but no one had the energy to take charge. By the time Jocelyn had finished it felt as though there was no one else in the room. It was just her and Kenneth. While she had known all these years they were only half siblings, she wondered what it must be like for him to suddenly have to absorb this information. Would he still think of her as his little sister or would she lose him now? And even as she wondered, he turned from her and stared at the fire once again.

Jocelyn's knees were hurting, but she stayed where she was, partly because she wanted to be of comfort to Kenneth, but also because she didn't want to see the others; didn't want to see whatever feelings and judgments they might be struggling with and, more than anything, did not want to feel the shame when she looked at Charles. Shame, and its sudden heat, surprised her, having been buried along with the secret; shame that she was the offspring of parents whose sordid submission to lust had allowed the one to betray his wife and the other to betray her sister; these two people, now and forevermore, her parents.

Instead, she reached for Kenneth's hand. "I'm so sorry you had to find out like this," she said.

Kenneth turned from the fire, his eyes devoid of any warmth he might have absorbed from its dying flames.

"Like this?" he said. "Like *this* would have been a treat. I knew long before you did. I knew before anyone." And pulling his hand out of Jocelyn's he unfolded the tired length of himself from the chair and abruptly left the room.

"Ken!" Jocelyn called after him. "What do you mean, you knew?" She struggled up off her knees but, looking somewhat defeated, sat in Kenneth's vacated chair. "If it's all right with everyone, I'd like to forfeit my turn with God. I've never believed in any God. End of story."

She found the handkerchief she had tucked up her sleeve, and swept away a tear. "But I do bloody believe in goodness. So, Sarah, if your God is good, maybe he can help you out. I suggest you get off your drunken arse and go see if you can mend the bridge to what's left of your marriage."

11

....

When Kenneth left the room he had no idea where to go. Not only in regard to his immediate surroundings, but in what now seemed to be the wasteland of his life. For a man who loved maps and had the ability to read them with an unerring sense of direction, he felt now, as he stood in the reception area of the inn, completely at a loss; he felt that he had no inner compass; that he had never known the true north of his life; hadn't, until this moment even contemplated its necessity.

Kenneth remembered the sweet, obedient boy he had been. A bit of a loner, never having had many friends, he'd nonetheless been content in his own world of model airplanes and bike rides. He'd been the kind of boy who, while never the teacher's pet, was well liked by them precisely because he did what he was told and for the most part did it well, if not with brilliance.

He considered the first fifteen years of his life to have been uneventful, but he had found comfort in the traditions and rhythms of Christmases and summer holidays with his parents; parents who, although lacking in outward displays of affection with him or each other, had nonetheless provided some modicum of safety for a child growing up. And if the house seemed hollow at the core, if the absence of laughter and spontaneity had an edge of unspoken sadness to it, it had also supported his innate need for solitary adventure.

The only extremes in Kenneth's life as a boy were between

the hours he spent in his tiny bedroom with his model planes and the hours he spent exploring the countryside on his bike. Yet there was almost no difference for him between the interior and exterior. He was content holed up in his room studying the instructions for building a plane; the subsequent concentration on careful cutting of the balsa wood, the assemblage of the parts, the taut application of thin-as-tissue paper over the skeleton and the final glossy coat of paint, just as he was content cycling down a country lane, an apple and a bar of chocolate in his saddle-bag. He'd loved the sensation of the hedgerows whizzing by over which he could glimpse horses and sheep, England's ancient trees and once in a while the distant shimmer of the sea. The only difference between the two states was the *fantasy* of freedom he experienced each time he took the most recent plane out for its maiden voyage, as opposed to the *reality* of freedom he felt when pedaling alone through the world. And, while he lived in hopes that one day one of his planes would survive its first flight without crashing to the ground, neither was it lost on him that he was a more able pilot of his bike, having not once fallen off it since the day he learned to ride it.

Kenneth sat on the edge of the armchair next to the grand-father clock, the memory of happy, carefree days evaporating as he remembered the summer his Aunt Jean stayed with them. Ten years younger than Kenneth's mother, Jean's first marriage had ended barely before it had begun and she had sought refuge with them until, as she liked to say, she had it sorted.

Kenneth didn't really like his aunt. There was something reck-less about her that frightened him. And he didn't like the way she teased him, commenting on how cute he was and how he should get a different haircut. "Get with it, Kenny," she would say and he'd recoil, not only from the abbreviation of his name, which he found cheap and undignified, but from some implicit threat of what might happen if he did "get with it." And he didn't like the way she tipped the balance in their family, as if four were the odd number, not three.

His mother spent her afternoons with the Women's Guild, or volunteering at the library, returning home at five each day to prepare dinner—Aunt Jean insisted she was hopeless in the kitchen. Kenneth's dad would usually get home from work around six. Unwilling to spend time alone with his aunt, Kenneth took to even longer bike rides that summer.

The front tyre had punctured twenty minutes after he left the house that afternoon and although he knew how to fix it, he found he was out of patches in his repair kit. Besides, he'd need to get the tyre off and put the inner tube in a bucket of water in order to find where the puncture was. It had taken him nearly an hour to walk the bike home and he was thirsty by the time he got there, so he'd propped the bike outside and let himself in the back door.

The sounds had frightened him, like someone was in pain. They were coming from upstairs but he couldn't figure what was going on. He'd crept up the stairs, heart wild in his chest, wondering if he'd have to rescue, or maybe even kill someone. But when he got to his parents' bedroom, he saw that not only was he not needed but that he needed not to be there. The image that greeted him filled him with horror: his father's naked back, the corded muscles of his neck, the thrust of his buttocks, his aunt's painted toenails, her thighs gripping his father's waist, her neck arched on the pillow, his mother's slippers neatly placed by the side of bed, all of it in colour and dimension beyond anything he'd ever seen. The image would be etched forever on his mind so that he would never in his life be able to make love without that image surfacing.

Kenneth stood up, peered down a dark hallway and began to weep.

12

Karenza was no stranger to witnessing other people's pain and while a part of her wanted to get the hell out—it was all too uncomfortably familiar—there was a side of her that wanted to see how it would all turn out. Apart from in her own family, she'd never seen this much pain in the lives of others.

She watched Sarah stagger out of the room with Jocelyn's eyes keenly fixed on her. Although she didn't want to admit it, she recognized something of herself in Sarah. Karenza was an outsider too, she and her parents having been blow-ins from Liverpool, not "natives." And it didn't take a genius to see that Sarah was a misfit even within her own family group. At least Karenza had been the longed-for daughter—something she suspected was not the same in Sarah's case. But perhaps, in part, it was all the attention her mother had lavished on her that had led to her father's resentment. That, and the gradual erosion of his self-esteem. Despite moving down here after the shipyards started closing, his career on the mackerel boats hadn't fared much better. Karenza had never known her father as the young optimist her mum had fallen in love with. She had only known him out of work, bitter and angry. The rows had started when she was too young to understand the words but old enough to be frightened by their tone. His voice lacerated by booze and smoke. A voice that penetrated her even when she hid under her bed, her little fingers stuffed in her ears while she sang *baa, baa, black sheep*. And it didn't help that once she started school she immediately outshone her twin brothers who, five years her senior, were already well on their way to delinquency.

By the time she was in her early teens and continuing to excel as a student, her father began to turn his resentment on her, as if she taunted him with her success. She came to dread him coming home from the pub. Who did Karenza think she was, flaunting her report cards, a soloist in the school choir, and now practising ballet; prancing around in her tights and what have you? Breasts already out there, skirts up to her arse.

Her dad could hold his liquor, that was one thing he could still do well. And he was holding a lot of it when Karenza came home from ballet class one day. He didn't think twice about following her into her room, pushing her onto the bed, face down, the swift entry into the narrow slit; it only ever took a few strokes and he'd be done, always from behind, always with his hand over her mouth and always the whispered promise to kill her if she told her mother.

Karenza shivered and shut down the thought, just as she had learned to shut herself down when her father forced his way into her. She looked around the lounge and wondered what was going on with Kenneth and Sarah. That was a conversation she'd like to hear.

"So," she said, to no one in particular, "this is a fun game. We're only on the first subject and two of us have already been eliminated."

"Don't be so sure," Jocelyn said. "People are known to come back stronger after a bit of a licking." She hoped this would be the case with her brother and sister-in-law. The shock of what had just transpired was beginning to lessen and now that it was all out in the air she realised she was experiencing the kind of relief one feels when a balloon pops, having known all along that it must, eventually. It was as though she had been holding her breath all these years and could finally take in more oxygen, whereas she knew that the ramifications for Sarah and Kenneth were only just beginning.

Jocelyn returned to Charles's side and leaned in to him. She was unsure how he'd be feeling other than shocked after learning the magnitude of the piece of Jocelyn's withheld history, but the arm that he extended around her shoulder suggested, nonetheless, that he was feeling protective of her. Or maybe he was just reassuring himself that she was still his Jocelyn and not somehow alchemically altered?

Tom was standing with his back to the fire which he had just stoked, laying on a couple of small logs to get it going again.

"It will be interesting to see what the next belief is, and who it belongs to, won't it?" he said.

"Oh, I don't think we should continue, do you?" Jocelyn asked.

"Oh, we must," Tom said. "I mean, apart from the fact that it's entertaining it would hardly be fair to stop after only one person. Don't you think that would make your sister-in-law feel rather picked upon?"

"Huh," Karenza snorted. "For someone being picked upon she certainly got even, didn't she?"

"That's not very fair, really," Jocelyn said. "After all, I'm the one who burdened her with it for all these years. I just can't believe that Ken knew about it all along . . . how ironic is it that we all knew."

"Well, I didn't," Charles said.

Jocelyn felt herself go cold. She recognized the tone in his voice. It was his default mode when feeling hurt to sound disapproving and she had to remind herself that he was hearing all of this for the first time. Why hadn't she told him? She'd told him everything else about her past and there had been a lot to tell, and much of it hard to say. She'd gone into the whole sleazy business. Not just the drinking, but the things she'd done as a result of it. How at first she drank to numb the pain of the family secret, that it had given her the false courage to ridicule her father until the day he nearly hit her, prompting her to leave home at sixteen. Then there was the first of her three husbands. She'd eloped with him to New York but he'd left her within nine months of their arrival. She drank always to get drunk, always to eradicate memory and any inhibition that might stand in the way of painting. And then the years of waitressing in jazz clubs, at one with the music, the smoke, the musicians, especially the drummers who fucked her in six-eight time. Nights of painting until dawn, managing to get Mimi fed and dressed for school before sleeping the day away. She'd stopped drinking for a year when she was pregnant and nursing and then, like all alcoholics who get sober for someone other than themselves, gradually slid back into the bottle, only now that she had a child, hiding it. She was a single parent by the time Mimi was a year old, having left the father, husband number two, because he wasn't spontaneous enough for her. She married number three because he bought one of her paintings at her first Manhattan show and, having drunk her way through the opening, took it as a sign that they were meant to be together. Not six weeks later, she'd come home early from a shift and found him masturbating on her daughter's bed, Mimi thankfully away for the weekend with her father. Jocelyn would never forget the image of him wearing her bra and a pair of her high-heels. She said nothing, merely turned, left the apartment, spent the night with a friend and quietly started divorce proceedings the next day. She'd continued to drink for another ten years, somehow managing to function, in total denial of having a problem and convinced she was a great mother.

All of this Charles knew. Within a week of their meeting each other she had told him everything; everything but this.

"Why didn't you tell me?" Charles asked his voice now sounding more confused than angry.

"Oh darling, I don't know. Really, I don't," she grabbed his hand in both of hers. "I've never told anyone except for Sarah. And frankly I managed to blank that out. Maybe I never got over the shock of finding out. I don't know. I was sixteen. It completely freaked me out. Like I lost my identity and the new one was horrifying," she paused for a moment. "And I think I was frightened that if I told you about this as well it would just be too much and you wouldn't want me." By now she was struggling to hold back tears. "I've always felt so ashamed."

"But Jocelyn, don't you see?" He looked at her in absolute amazement. "This is the one thing you *weren't* responsible for."

13

....

When Sarah left the lounge she felt like a teenager who'd been sent to Coventry by her friends. She would like to have crawled into the first bed she could find and taken a sleeping pill to wake up cleansed of memory the next morning, but her pills were back at their hotel on the harbour. She sat down on the loveseat opposite the reception desk and tried to think of a way out: out of the inn, out of her marriage, maybe even out of her life. Although the wind and rain were still constant it wasn't quite as loud as it had been in the lounge. This must be the sheltered side, Sarah thought, and nearly laughed out loud at the absurd thought that shelter existed anywhere.

As her ears became accustomed to the relative silence she heard a mewling sound coming from the end of the hallway to the right. Having never heard Kenneth cry during their thirty years of marriage it never occurred to her that it was him. Instead, her addled brain told her it must be a cat frightened by the storm, and being a cat lover and glad of a distraction, she went off in search of something she might comfort.

The hall was dark and unable to find the light switch she groped her way along. She had almost reached the end when she saw Kenneth. He was sitting on the floor, legs out in front of him, back slumped against the wall. She watched him for a moment, saw his bowed head, his shoulders rounded over his sobbing chest and it was as though she became riven; one half of her wanting to hurry to him, to hold him, to comfort him, the other half wanting to flee. When was the last time either of them had held the other? When had either of them ever asked for or given comfort? And why would he want anything from her now, after what she'd just done? And anyway, what comfort had he ever been to her? Did he think patting her hand and muttering there, there, after every miscarriage could be categorized as comfort? Where had he been when their dead child slid out of her like a stone? Not wanting to be a burden to him, she had done her crying alone in the army hospital. When he came to take her home she asked to stop at the pet shop where he reluctantly agreed to buy a kitten, and then he soldiered on while she began her retreat into alcohol and sleeping pills.

She had no idea where she was headed when she turned from him and began groping her way back down the hall, sure that just like in the rest of their lives together he hadn't seen her. His disembodied voice shocked her.

"If you leave now it will be the end of us," he said.

His words went into her like an arrow that had been arcing towards her since the day they married, his statement carrying a finality that was strangely lacking in weight. She turned to him, agony making itself felt in spite of the booze.

"But we never really began, did we?" she said and sliding down the wall, she sat there, six feet from him and sobbed.

14

....

"Right," Karenza said. "I reckon we could all do with some tea and toast." She turned to Tom, "How about giving me a hand?"

"Sounds like a good idea," he said.

"Do you want us to help?" Jocelyn asked.

"No, we'll be fine, thanks," Karenza said. "You two keep the home fire burning."

When Karenza and Tom left the room, Jocelyn got up and closed the door behind them, while Charles went to the fire and placed some more logs on it, fanning the flames with the book Kenneth had been reading.

"Remind me not to consider a career in the invention of parlour games," Jocelyn said, trying to break the tension between them.

"Oh, I don't know," Charles said, his back still towards her. "I'd say this is one game everyone should play."

"What do you mean?"

"Well, it's like taking a truth serum. We've only had one round so far, but it looks like we might find out in the end that belief has nothing to do with truth."

"Yes, but we don't want to demolish each other with truth, do we?"

"Do you think I've been demolished?" Charles asked, turning to her.

"Maybe not demolished but hurt," she said.

"I'm a big boy, Jocelyn. It would take more than the sin of omission to wipe me out. Unless there's something else you've omitted to tell me that would have a direct bearing on our relationship."

"Like what?'

"Well, I don't know . . . like if you've ever been unfaithful to me."

"For God's sake, Charles . . ."

"Don't bring him into it!"

A shared laugh brought them a moment's respite.

"I'm sorry, Charles. Not just that I didn't tell you about this before, but it feels like I've broken some trust. Why else would you be asking me if I've ever been unfaithful?"

"Come on, I wasn't being serious," he said, gesturing with his hand as though he was batting away an unwelcome thought. But in fact, he realized that Jocelyn's withholding of something on that scale did make him suddenly wonder if she was capable of withholding other information.

"Yes you were," she said. "You were serious, and I don't blame you. I know I've done some damage."

Charles got up from the fire and put his arms around her. "The real damage was done to you, years ago," he said. "Whatever ding we've suffered tonight can be repaired with a little time." He kissed her forehead and gathered her into him.

"Talking about time," she said, pulling away a little, "It's been a while since Kenneth and Sarah left. Do you think we should go and see how they're doing?"

"I'd leave them to it for a little longer, Joss. They've got a lot to talk about." Jocelyn and Charles went back to the couch and watched the fire as it blazed in the grate. Whatever bump in the road they had just hit, it was nothing compared to the bomb that had landed in the barren terrain of Kenneth and Sarah's marriage. Charles tolerated the occasional visits to England because he knew how much Kenneth meant to Jocelyn. He liked Kenneth well enough, thought he was a decent man saddled with a less than wonderful wife. Charles couldn't fathom their marriage at all, couldn't imagine what kept them together beyond denial and a lack of courage to go for anything better. God knows how it was for Kenneth day in day out—he found being around Sarah so difficult, aware each time they were all together, that her drinking would result in some inappropriate comment. Her jealousy of Jocelyn was barely disguised after a few drinks. There was no doubt it was awkward.

Jocelyn was poking at the fire distractedly still trying to digest the enormity of what had just happened. She knew how the lie she had grown up with had affected her, and how the secrecy had additionally distorted reality. Yet while she could never excuse her father's behaviour, or her real mother's abandonment of her, she had found some measure of compassion for them. Perhaps it was the relief of confession, or the perspective of having led a less than perfect life. But then the feeling of relief was overruled by a sudden realization.

"Oh, no," she said, turning to Charles with a stricken look on her face.

"What is it, darling?"

"It's just dawned on me. Ken said he knew before anyone."

Charles looked at her, and she saw he didn't get it.

"Don't you see? That means he must have seen them fucking! God." She tried to imagine how awful that must have been. To have witnessed that at the tender age of fifteen? Only now could she begin to get a glimpse of how experiencing that might have shaped his entire view of sex and marriage. This changed everything. Maybe this was why he had fought his parents so hard to join the army. It wasn't courage he'd sought, but the repression of feelings. Suddenly his choice of Sarah as a wife made sense. Sweet and pretty as Sarah may have been when Kenneth first met her, she had never given off any sexual heat. She was a vicar's daughter for God's sake. An image came to her, of the two of them when they met, thirty years ago; two lost souls finding safety in each other's remove.

Jocelyn reached for Charles's hand. "They need help," she said. "We need to help them."

15

Tom watched as Karenza made her way around the kitchen as though it were her own; first filling an electric urn with water and switching it on, then to the bread bin for a loaf of granary and on to the fridge for cheese. She'd put her hair up in one of those makeshift buns that young women are so adept at, a careless look that he knew was well practiced. One wavy strand had escaped and was caressing her neck like a pale gold serpent while two others coiled at her temples.

"Here," she said, brandishing a serrated knife in his direction, "start slicing. Not too thin, but don't make doorsteps either. It's got to last."

"Yes ma'am," he said, and she laughed, the sound of it after all the recent tension seemed almost indecent and yet filled him with relief. "God," he said, and hearing the word, laughed himself. "Just can't get away from him can we?"

"Speak for yourself. What were you going to say?"

"I was going to say it's good to get out of the lounge."

"Yeah, bit of an oxymoron there, eh?"

"What do you mean?"

"Lounging was hardly what was going on there."

"You can say that again. It's enough to put you off marriage all together," Tom said and winced as an image of Lily came to mind.

"Looks like you got lucky then," Karenza said.

"How's that?'

"Maybe your lady love did you a favour when she jilted you."

Tom turned back to the business of slicing. In his professional life he dealt with tension on an almost daily basis whether in conferences between competitive clients, courtroom appearances, or the fluctuation of the markets. Yet he was always able to distance himself from the tension and as a result was often the most powerful person in the room. But emotional tension was a minefield for him. It was one of the reasons he'd fallen for Lily; her lack of personal drama, her practical, no-nonsense approach to life, which allowed her to come from a place of assertion rather than aggression. If it made her a little boring in bed, what matter, sexual fantasy was easy to superimpose. What Tom wanted in a wife was constancy and loyalty and Lily had been rich in those qualities.

"Penny for your thoughts," Karenza said.

Tom kept slicing. "It'll cost you a lot more than that," he said. Anxious to change the subject he asked, "What about you, do you have a love interest?"

"Nope, and I'm not interested in love. There's another load of crap for you, just like God."

"You're a prickly girl, aren't you?" he said, handing her a stack of sliced bread which she began inserting into three professional toasters.

"Interesting choice of adjective," she said, and when he looked at her with a frown she enlightened him. "Prickly. Words are fascinating aren't they? Women are prickly; men are pricks." She handed him a large earthenware crock of butter, "Why don't you show me what a smooth prick you are and spread this?"

He watched her as she flitted away to the other side of the kitchen to warm two large teapots. A long butcher block island ran down the centre of the kitchen stranding them on either side of it.

Tom started buttering the toast; the sound of the knife scraping on the crisp surface reminded him of all the late Sunday mornings that his father had made breakfast trays to take up to Tom's mother in a valiant effort at rallying her. It was another one of those indulgences his father bestowed on his mother, along with the lavish gifts—maybe this was why Tom had spent an obscene amount of money on Lily's ring. He and his dad would have had a full English breakfast hours earlier, the two of them eating in silence. On his return from Sunday school, Tom would hear the scrape of the knife before he even got in the kitchen door and it would set his teeth on edge, the way the tolling of the church bell for the eleven o'clock service did, the two sounds forming brackets between which the failure of repentance and the obliteration of hope lay trapped.

As he buttered the last slice, he wondered if the comfort that so many people associated with the smell of toast could possibly salve the wounds of the strangers for whom he now prepared it.

"What do you think Kenneth and Sarah are up to?" he asked.

"Sucking each other's thumbs in a dark crevice probably."

"I thought I was jaded, but I'm a novice compared to you."

"I could give you lessons after school if you like," giving him a sassy look over her shoulder while still slicing cheddar cheese off a huge block.

"Sounds worse than detention," Tom said. "Does your after-school curriculum extend to anything more sporting?"

She'd come over to the cupboards on his side of the island to get plates, cups and saucers. She turned and, pressing herself into him from behind, reached for his crotch, "Something like this?" she asked. He turned to kiss her, but she stepped aside, put the crockery on a tray and went back to the other side of the kitchen where she spooned tea leaves into the pots before adding the now scalding water from the urns, while Tom stood immobilized, aroused and humiliated.

Karenza finished assembling the toast and cheese on a large platter, which she placed on a tray with the teapots, and then having already put the dishes on another tray handed it to Tom. "Here," she said. "Time to feed the animals."

16

Kenneth was still slumped against the wall listening to Sarah mewling. His ultimatum had issued from him like a piece of phlegm he'd been trying to clear from his throat for years without knowing it. The truth, now expelled, seemed to reverberate in the darkness while the echo of Sarah's statement careened off the walls; two solitary sentences twinned with truth and sorrow.

How did one end what had never begun? What had they never begun? What exactly had they been doing for the last thirty years? Had Sarah wanted something different, and if so what was it? What had he failed at? It wasn't his fault they were childless. He'd never wanted children anyway; what was the point of bringing more suffering into the world? He knew Sarah had suffered with every loss, only natural for a woman. But he'd done his best to fill the void, had built the conservatory she'd dreamed of, taken them on holidays to the continent, redecorated the house countless times at her whim, fancy meals in a good restaurant once a week. They owned their house, had no debt. Why couldn't she be grateful for what they had instead of mourning what they lacked? Why couldn't she grow up and accept that you just couldn't have everything you wanted in life?

"I want to go home," she cried.

"You always want what you can't have," Kenneth snapped. "That's your problem, that and your bloody drinking and your ridiculous ideas about faith. Look where that's got us."

"And you're blameless, I suppose," she retorted. "It must be very handy for you to have such a failure for a wife, someone you can quietly blame for everything without ever having to take a look at your own shit, you self-righteous bastard."

The shock of hearing Sarah utter *shit* and *bastard* in the same sentence caused Kenneth to stifle a snort. "Actually, it's not me who's the bastard but Jocelyn, as you so kindly let everyone know."

Kenneth couldn't see her face, but the ensuing silence hinted at the remorse Sarah was more than likely feeling. "Are you going to leave me?" she asked, eventually.

Kenneth felt the familiar undertow, the booze-sodden contrition that Sarah had used all these years as a way of hauling him in. And he'd always reached for the end of the rope, a drowning man clinging to hope.

"I don't know," he said, getting to his feet. As he walked the six feet that separated them, he felt the immeasurable distance that they had complicitly, if unconsciously, created over the years of their marriage. He had no idea how, or if, it could ever be bridged, but like the good soldier he was, he did the decent thing for now and helped Sarah to her feet.

They entered the reception area at the same time as Jocelyn and Charles, the four of them halting at the sight of each other as if they'd come across strangers in the desert.

"We were just coming to get you," Jocelyn said, as though they were picking up children from school. The awkward silence was interrupted by the clatter of the swing door to the kitchen. Tom, holding a large tray, was backing out through the door in order to keep it open for Karenza. The two of them stopped when they saw the other four, all of them eyeing each other for a clue as to what to say or do next.

"Right," Karenza said, breaking the tension. "Anyone fancy a bit of sustenance?"

Charles held the door to the lounge open as everyone filed in. Only in England, he thought, was it possible to come this close to carnage only to stop for tea and toast, as though nothing had happened. But then this was a nation that had managed to dance in the streets while their homes were being bombed. Still, he thought, it was a treacherous line between courage and denial.

The trays were placed on the sideboard and everyone stood there bereft of a familiar role.

"Shall I pour?" Jocelyn offered.

"That would be brilliant," Karenza retied her hair, deftly gathering the escaping strands back into her topknot. "Shall I ring Trevor? See if there's any news?"

"Do you want me to wait until you get back?" Jocelyn asked.

"No, I'll just be a few minutes."

"Let me help," Sarah said, anxious for something to do. The last drink was beginning to wear off and she wished she could find a way of adding a splash to her tea without being seen.

"Come and help yourself to milk and sugar, and there's cheese on toast for those who want it."

Sarah grimaced but then smiling weakly said, "That would be lovely." Jocelyn noticed her glance over to Kenneth whose sense of decorum would normally have had him serving his wife, but he remained resolutely in his chair. Charles began to get up from the couch but Jocelyn waved him back, "Sit darling, I'll get yours."

Tom watched the two couples. How different they were: the one, together for decades, so obviously never really together and now possibly on the brink of an irrevocable split; and the other couple, with much less time under their belts and perhaps with some rough patches in need of repair, yet so obviously willing to go the distance. He wondered which category he and Lily would have fitted into. As soon as the question arose he knew that the distance that had already existed between them, both physically and emotionally, was the reason Lily had rejected him. He couldn't help but feel piqued with resentment of Charles and Jocelyn.

He looked over to poor old Kenneth, who having busied himself with the fire, was now devouring three slices of toasted cheese and was already on his second cup of very strong tea as though he'd done a hard day's work on a building site. Tom found it within himself to sympathise with the guy, despite feeling vaguely nauseated by what he saw as his lack of backbone. Jocelyn was the last to be seated and Tom watched her as she blew the steam from her mug, all the while gazing at her brother. He could read the pain in her eyes. Nothing like a bit of public humiliation to bring out sibling loyalty, he thought, with only a trace of scorn.

He was saved from further contemplation by Karenza's return, who, looking at Charles, said, "Well, as you Americans would say, we are shit out of luck. Emergency Services won't be here for at least another couple of hours." As if to make that perfectly clear the grandfather clock out in reception chimed ten sonorous strokes.

When it finished, Karenza said, "Well, that gives us until midnight before we change into pumpkins."

"I think some of us already have," Tom quipped.

"Well then," Jocelyn retorted. "It gives you time to change into something with a less bitter rind."

Karenza poured herself a cup of milky tea and walked over to the drinks trolley. "I fancy a splash of brandy in mine, anyone else?"

"Oh, that would be lovely," Sarah said rather too quickly, having immediately convinced herself that as long as someone else was having a drop then really, what was the harm?

Kenneth looked at her in brief disbelief, the disbelief vanishing before it took root in denial. He turned to the fire, the feeling of futility that he'd repressed all these years burning into him now. He had an impulse to put his hand in the flames, to brand himself with this knowledge lest it be erased by sleep.

"So, now that we're fortified, let's carry on with the game," said Tom. "We've got God out the way, so it should be a doddle."

"Oh, I don't think . . ." Jocelyn began before Kenneth interrupted her.

"I agree with Tom," he said. "And besides, why shouldn't everyone else have a chance at being demolished."

Jocelyn looked at her brother. She saw his quiet fury and although she knew he was in pain, felt that there was some hope for him; maybe the fury might burn through his avoidance of truth. Now that the truth of their family secret was out perhaps he could spend the energy he'd used for protecting his little sister and insulating himself from feeling, to pursue the sense of adventure he'd had as a boy.

Charles interrupted her thoughts. "Why don't we vote on it? Those in favour raise your hands."

Five hands shot up, leaving Jocelyn with both of hers around her mug.

"So, who's going to choose the next one?" Karenza asked.

"Oh, it should be Sarah," Charles said. He took the vase off the mantel and passed it to her. "Give it a good shake."

> PART II <

17

....

"It says here 'Impermanence,'" Sarah said, grateful that it was written big enough that she could read it without her glasses. She seemed to have misplaced her handbag.

"Wow," Jocelyn said. "Another biggie. Is 'impermanence' a belief? Whose is it, anyway?'

"Mine," Charles said.

Jocelyn looked at him as if he'd made a mistake. "Really?" she asked.

"Yes," he said, looking down at his teacup. A look of confusion briefly crossed Jocelyn's face, as though perhaps it was she who had made a mistake, so that suddenly she wasn't quite sure who he was.

Noticing this, Tom lost some of his resentment. It was as though he was watching what had passed between him and Lily, for in the moment when Lily had closed the lid and pushed the little box back to his side of the table he was at first more ashamed of having made such a huge mistake than he was hurt by the rejection.

"Well, Charles," he said. "You've got my vote right off the bat. But I'd like to hear you explain what you mean by impermanence."

"Well, it's pretty obvious, isn't it? Nothing, I mean nothing, lasts forever."

"What about plastic molecules," Karenza chirped in, clearly enjoying the conundrum. "Aren't they forever?"

"OK, fair point, but then you'd have to believe in the permanence of the universe."

"Are you saying that you don't?" Karenza asked.

"Yes."

"Wow, you'd think the dawn of a new millennium would make you think of beginnings not endings. That's awesome."

"What's awesome about it?" Jocelyn asked.

"Well, it's so, I don't know, so final. I mean what is there to say? OK. Everything ends. Maybe that's a good thing."

"Really?" The emotion was rising in Jocelyn's voice. "You think everything ends? You think suffering ends, how about poverty? You think evil ends? How about love?" she asked, turning to Charles. "Is that impermanent too?" She cut herself off, just short of asking the question that was screaming in her head. Is *that* why you don't want to get married? Are we part of your belief in impermanence? Steadying herself, she diverted her comments elsewhere. "I mean, really Charles, of all the things there are to believe in; evolution, progress, compassion, forgiveness, redemption, love for chrissakes, you choose impermanence? What about a cure for cancer, do you believe in that?"

"Not completely, there will always be some form of cancer."

"Then doesn't that make cancer permanent?" Tom challenged.

"No, because cancer dies with the person. Look," he said, turning to Jocelyn, "it's not that I don't believe in love or any of the things you said, but none of them are permanent because we all die. To me, if you're talking about any kind of belief it has to be based in fact, and the only fact I know for sure is that everything ends."

"But it's so impersonal," Jocelyn said, unable to hide her dismay.

"Maybe that's the best kind of belief to have," said Kenneth, as though the prospect of impermanence offered a comforting way out. After all, he'd kept a secret all these years believing that it would remain a secret permanently. And look where that had gotten him.

"But setting aside that we all die in the end, don't you think people do permanent, irreparable damage to each other?" Karenza asked.

"You mean like if someone loses their legs in a car accident for example?" Charles asked.

"Yeah, that or I don't know, psychological damage?"

"I suppose you could argue permanent damage has been done, but it is possible to choose to live an undamaged life and even those who don't, eventually die."

"I had no idea you were such a cold bastard," Jocelyn said, and for the first time in a long while wished she could have a drink.

"Why are you so upset?" Charles asked. "You're the one who says everyone has a right to their beliefs without being judged. Correct me if I'm wrong but I feel like you're judging me, which rather proves the impermanence of your so-called belief in 'live and let live.'"

Cornered, Jocelyn got up and went to the sideboard for a refill of tea. This happened between them often, this kind of argument where they used each other's words for ammunition, the back and forth of which made it almost impossible to follow the thread back to the original thought or question. Charles was the only person she'd met who was as good at this as she was and there were times when these escalating volleys ripped them apart leaving them exhausted and doubting their relationship. But she loved that they were always able to find their way back to each other and in the process learn more about the wounds they still carried and the ways in which they defended against being hurt.

As she poured milk into her tea, she reflected that Charles probably thought like this because of all the loss he and his family had suffered. It made sense, but nonetheless she felt anxious about how it might affect their future. It hadn't occurred to her at the start of the evening that she might be contemplating the sustainability of the relationship she had with the man she loved.

18

....

Jocelyn took her tea, walked past Charles and curled up on the window seat again. The storm, as if in opposition to this idea of impermanence, had redoubled its energy and peering through the panes, Jocelyn could see that several small branches had been ripped off the large pine tree. An occasional streak of lightning fizzed over the sea, but the sky had lost its thunder, as had the inhabitants of the lounge.

Sarah, apparently having nothing to say on the subject of impermanence, had nodded off in her chair. Her face, smoothed by slumber, betrayed traces of the young woman Kenneth had married. Yet the more he looked at her now the more he wondered what on earth had attracted him to her. Certainly it hadn't been sexual. If anything, it had been that she was asexual. It's not that he had never felt sexual attraction, he'd just never been able to act on it, the act itself permanently associated with his father's betrayal. The irony of his sex life with Sarah was that on the infrequent occasions they had intercourse she'd become pregnant almost every time. That the pregnancies always ended in death seemed hardly surprising to him now; how could anything created in such a void possibly hope to survive?

As it was, Kenneth had thought he must have held some sort of record for masturbation—starting the summer of his aunt's visit. In spite of repulsing him she'd confused him thrice a day in the privacy of his room where his fantasies of touching her had overcome him as he touched himself. He flushed as he remembered the feelings of revulsion and shame he'd suffered subsequent to witnessing her with his father. This had done nothing to stop his need to masturbate; he just switched the object of his fantasy to the girl in his class whom he deemed to be the most pure. Sarah, the vicar's daughter. So maybe that was it? Maybe that's why he'd married Sarah. To escape the feelings of guilt and dirtiness. Except that, as is so often the case, reality hadn't measured up to fantasy. Kenneth had only ever been able to get an erection by fantasizing about women who looked far from pure. The memory of Karenza sashaying across the lounge in those boots flashed into his mind, jolting him suddenly back into the room.

He drained his tea, wondering if Charles's theory of the impermanence of damage might extend to him or whether he was the exception that proved the rule.

Tom got up, stretched and sauntered over to the sideboard. He felt the teapot to see if it was still hot. Cool to his touch, he took an after dinner mint instead and as he unwrapped it turned to Charles and Jocelyn.

"Come on, you two. You're not going to fall out over this are you?" Neither was looking at the other, and it was impossible not to notice the *froideur* between them. "You know what?" he popped the mint in his mouth. "I think it is perfectly possible to be logical and scientific about life *and* to be warm and human at the same time." Charles shrugged and smiled at Tom in recognition of his attempt at mediation, but Jocelyn's seaward gaze suggested she wasn't ready to relent just yet.

"Yeah, come on guys, we've hardly got going," Karenza seemed eager to continue the sport. "It's a really interesting idea, I just wonder where it comes from." She moved towards Charles and sat on the floor next to his chair. A strand of hair caught on her eyelashes as she looked up at him. "Were you orphaned at birth or something?" she asked flippantly, blowing at the stray hair flirtatiously.

"Christ," Tom said. "You don't beat about the bush! Do you plan on becoming a shrink or a lawyer?"

"A lawyer," she replied, her statement, travelling around the room like a boomerang, even jolted Sarah from her nap.

"You must be joking," Tom said, giving a derisive hoot.

"You're a superior bastard, aren't you," she said, kicking a booted leg in his direction. "You think you've got everything all sized up at first glance, don't you? I saw the way you looked at me when I served your dinner. Your condescension preceded you." She turned from him and addressed the others.

"I'm not just an ignorant little local girl, dropped out of school, waiting tables until I get pregnant. I know how to play the game. The more superior I make you feel, the bigger the tips. So don't give me any of your social stereotyping, OK?"

Jocelyn, watching her from across the room, admired the girl's pluck and her ability to read people. "Good for you. I'm sure you're right," she admitted. "It's very easy to make assumptions about people. You'll make a great lawyer, I'm sure."

"So, when do you plan on going to university?" Charles asked.

"Already there. I'm in my third year at Oxford," she said.

"You sure about that?" Tom continued his patronizing tack. "The Michaelmas term doesn't end for another couple of weeks. I should know, I went there myself."

"Not that it's any of your business, but I'm on a leave of absence to look after my mother who's recovering from hip surgery. She lives alone."

"Oh," Tom muttered.

"Good job you're not a lawyer," she said. "You need to do your homework before cross-examination."

"Actually, I am a lawyer," he said.

"Well, I'll be sure not to hire you if I ever need one," she retorted.

Sarah had been trying to follow the exchange as it went back and forth like a pingpong ball. But now she felt quite dizzy. Nothing was as it had seemed. It was like everyone was changing into someone else. She couldn't keep track of it all. She was still trying to figure out if impermanence meant there was no afterlife. Panic was on the rise again. Maybe she should have some toasted cheese after all. She tried to get up but wasn't sure she would make it and slumped back down again; she was afraid she'd fall and do herself permanent damage. She giggled to herself. Was it Charles who'd said there was no such thing as permanent damage? What did he know?

Seeing her struggling out of the corner of his eye, Charles took the opportunity to move the conversation on. "Can I get you something, Sarah?" he asked.

She looked at him gratefully, "How kind of you," she said. "I'd love some of that toast if there's any left."

"Don't forget to drizzle brandy on it," Kenneth added with uncustomary venom.

There was a moment of awkward silence before Karenza said, "So, Charles, you haven't answered my question."

"I really am on the stand!" Charles replied, looking distinctly as though he'd rather not be.

He handed Sarah her toast and while he was up, decided to put another log on the fire. It was the last one. Maybe by the time it was gone they all would be, too.

"As a matter of fact," he said, keeping his tone as light-hearted as he could, "my mother died while giving birth to me. And sure, that's had an enduring effect. But life ends. That's just the way it is. But I don't think it's this particularly that makes me dwell on the impermanence of things. And besides, I had a father who gave his all for me so . . ."

"So you *can* be permanently marked for life then," Karenza insisted, as if it was more important to catch him out than it was to register the enormity of what he'd just disclosed.

"What is it with women that you have to consistently twist our words. I am not *marked* for life. I'm sad I never knew my mother, but I hardly consider that permanent damage, especially, as I just said, I was well loved and provided for by my father."

By now, Jocelyn had been drawn away from the sea view and was perched on the edge of the window seat clearly enthralled by this exchange. She hated to admit it but she recognized in Karenza a side of herself she didn't like; the side that bullies men. In order to ... what? Gain the upper hand? Why? In order to maintain distance? A form of revenge? Certainly all of that applied to her in the relationships she'd had before she quit drinking. But why did she still do it with Charles?

"So, what happened to your dad?" Karenza asked.

"He died."

"Oh. When?'

"My first year of college," he said, poking at the fire.

"What did he die of?" Karenza asked.

"It was his heart, okay?" Charles snapped, still busying himself with the fire.

The relentlessness of Karenza's questioning finally got to Jocelyn. Wasn't it obvious to the girl that Charles clearly didn't want to discuss it?

"Karenza, why don't you just leave it?" she said, giving her a cold look.

Charles had never really wanted to discuss his father's death with Jocelyn. She had assumed that it had been one loss too many and respected his need to protect himself, hoping that one day he might feel safe enough to unburden himself. She got up and walked over to where he was kneeling by the fire and caressed the back of his head.

"Oh," she exclaimed, looking at the empty woodbin. "We need more logs. Are there more outside?" she asked, turning to Karenza.

"Yeah, there's a stack out by the car park. But you'll get drenched going out there in this weather."

"Can't we just let it die out and turn up the heat?" Sarah asked. Kenneth marveled at such an apt description of the current state of their marriage, yet was loath to see the fire end.

"Surely there must be umbrellas in the lobby," he said.

"You think you can keep them up in this wind?" Karenza looked at him like he was an idiot.

"We could use trash bags as raincoats," Charles suggested, glad of the distraction.

"Well, I'm not going out there," Karenza said, folding her arms.

"Leave it to us men," Tom said. "We still have our uses."

"You reckon?" Karenza said. She stood up and moved towards the door. "The bin-liners are in the pantry, I'll show you where they are."

"Bin-liners?" Charles asked.

"What do you call 'em, trash thingies?" Karenza said.

"Oh, trash bags. Gotcha," Charles said.

If *only*, she thought, as she reached for the door knob.

As the men headed out the door an enormous flash of lightning lit up the window followed by the sound of a large branch ripping itself free of the pine tree. Everyone froze, waiting for the inevitable crash which, when it came, pitched the entire inn into darkness.

19

....

"Oh, for fuck's sake," Karenza said grumpily. "What is this, a bloody Agatha Christie plot?"

"Right, well, let's get organized," Kenneth said. "First we need a torch, preferably a couple."

"There are two in the kitchen, in the pantry," Karenza said, "and a couple more in the handyman's cupboard in the hall. Oh, and there are candles in the pantry, too."

"Right-o," Kenneth said. "Tom, you were in the kitchen before. Can you visualize where the pantry is?"

"Yup. I know where it is."

"Why don't you take Charles with you and Karenza and I will go to the handyman's cupboard."

"Guess who got the short straw!" Tom quipped. "Come on then Charles. Are you feeling intrepid?"

"I hardly need assistance getting two torches," Karenza retorted. "Why don't you go with the boys and get the bin-liners from the pantry."

"Fine," Kenneth said, feeling somewhat demoted. "Then we'll all rendezvous in the lounge and figure out what comes next."

"Probably Jack Nicholson with an axe," Karenza said, as she headed down the hallway without a pause.

"Boy, she is one tough biscuit, that one," Tom spoke quietly, not wanting to be overheard by her. "Can't wait until we get to her turn. It's hard to imagine *what* she believes in—that's if she believes in anything at all. I'll lead the way, shall I?"

Although they were gradually getting adjusted to the dark, it wasn't easy negotiating the furniture but they shuffled off with Tom calling out directions and warnings. Once in the kitchen he yelled to Charles and Kenneth to watch out for the butcher block island. It was even darker in the pantry and almost impossible to distinguish between jars and tins, bottles and dishes, never mind finding the damn torches.

"Does anyone have a lighter?" Kenneth asked.

"Not me," Tom said.

"Me neither," said Charles.

"Is the stove gas or electric?" Kenneth asked.

"Haven't the foggiest," said Tom. "We didn't use it for the tea."

"Oh, it has to be gas," said Charles." It's a professional kitchen. Why?"

"Well, if it's gas we could light a twist of paper and . . ."

"Igniter won't work," Tom interrupted. "It'll be an electric sparker."

"Ah. Good point."

The pantry was roughly seven feet long by five wide with shelves on three sides. Following Kenneth's suggestion, they each took a side and began groping their way along as if in a game of blind man's bluff. Charles was the first to find a torch, but not before Tom had knocked over an industrial-sized jar of honey which, when it shattered on the floor, splattered a mixture of sticky goo and splintered glass, and before Charles was able to find the ON/OFF switch on his torch all three of them had managed to step in it. A slight sucking sound could be heard as each of them tried to lift their feet. "The Three Stooges to the rescue," Charles laughed.

"More like the three bears," Kenneth joked, feeling better than he had done in a long time.

"Wait till Goldilocks gets here," Tom said. "You won't be laughing then."

Having switched on the torch, Charles aimed its beam at the floor. "Christ," he said, "how are we going to get this off?"

"Uh, soap and water," Tom said sarcastically.

"No electricity ergo no hot water," Charles replied.

"So much for impermanence," Tom quipped.

"Aha," Kenneth exclaimed. "Here's the other torch. Oh, dead battery."

"Oh, well," Tom said. "Let's find the candles and bin-liners and get out of here."

"We could use the bags to cover our shoes," Kenneth said, sounding more like a boy scout that a retired military officer.

"Excellent thinking," Charles said.

They found three boxes; one containing white medium-sized bags used for the guests bathroom wastebaskets. Kenneth suggested they use these to cover their shoes, which they did after doing their best to pick off as much glass as possible and then securing them by folding the tops of their socks over them. They used two of the large bags for swag, throwing in packets of digestive biscuits, a box of cornflakes, a bag of raisins, two bars of baking chocolate and six bottles of still water. Kenneth found a large basket with several boxes of candles to which he added the two rolls of large plastic bags. Before leaving the scene of the crime they did a quick raid of the fridge denuding it of cheese, ham, and a jar of mustard. As they filed past the island the beam of the torch illuminated a bowl of pears, which Kenneth balanced on top of his wicker basket, the whole lot falling to the floor as Karenza pushed open the swing door from the other side, hitting him on the knuckles.

"What the fuck ..." she said, blinding them with her torch. Then, seeing their feet, she laughed so hard she had to cross her legs.

20

"What an astounding evening," Jocelyn said. "You couldn't make this up if you tried, could you?"

"Fiction is stranger than truth," Sarah mumbled.

"It's the other way around," Jocelyn said.

"Who cares? I can't tell the difference anymore."

If Sarah hadn't been so drunk, Jocelyn would have credited her with acute insight, instead she asked her if she was all right, a flabby question which she regretted as soon as it left her mouth.

"Oh, yes, I'm just *fine*, thank you. I'm stranded in a creepy inn on the edge of a cliff in a raging storm, there's no electricity, I've been ridiculed by strangers and am soon to be abandoned by my husband because I said out loud what you and he knew all along but never had the balls to discuss."

Jocelyn was familiar with the belligerent stage of boozing and knew it was useless to try and communicate with her. How many sodden nights had *she* spent spinning her tales of woe, exaggeration and repetition? Like so many drunks, she'd created an impenetrable wall of victimhood, which not only allowed for escape from responsibility, but led inevitably to requiring another drink and another, until futility was doused by a blackout that had nothing to do electricity and everything to do with an advanced stage of alcoholism. What irony, Jocelyn thought, that her sister-in-law was doubly powerless tonight. She tried to find the appropriate words of comfort, but knew how easily it could be taken for condescension. Better to change the subject.

"Well, let's hope the men have successfully raided the kitchen. They'll need to get the wood in soon if we're to keep this fire going."

"Oh, I'm sure Kenneth is in his element giving orders to everyone," Sarah said. "Unlike our marriage, this is a crisis he's well-equipped to handle." She managed to push herself up from the chair and, keeping her focus on the drinks trolley, wove her way over to it, poured a couple of inches into her teacup and rather than risk navigating the distance back to her armchair, plonked herself down on the window seat where she sagged amongst its cushions.

Jocelyn turned with relief as the door opened and Karenza, with a vaudevillian *ta-da*, and using the beam of her torch as a spotlight, presented the three musketeers who traipsed in like sheepish schoolboys caught in the act of petty thievery. Tom had his bag of goodies slung over his shoulder, Charles held his in front of him, while Kenneth carried his reassembled basket on his arm like a housewife from the fifties. And then she saw their feet.

"Oh, Sarah, look," she said. "The three blind mice."

And for a blessed moment everyone was united in mirth. And how easy it was in that first moment of shared hilarity, after all the personal revelations of past and present battles, to forget that, in fact, they were all now in a state of emergency.

The room was already losing its heat, the last log more than half-consumed and the radiators cold. It was Karenza who cracked the whip.

"Okay, time to get organized here." While the men made appropriate holes in the bin liners for heads and arms, Jocelyn and Karenza lit candles from the diminishing flames in the hearth and, using saucers as holders, placed a dozen of them around the room.

It would have to be said that whether Sarah was actually asleep or merely faking it, nobody really cared, preferring not to have to deal with her less-than-fully-functioning self, although Jocelyn did find it in her to cover her with the chenille blanket that had been draped over the arm of the couch.

As the men prepared to brave the elements, Jocelyn shone a torch on them, snorted and quickly covered her mouth with her hand finding it near impossible not to laugh. They were all roughly the same height and so the dark grey plastic bags, through which they had stuck their heads and arms, came down to just below their hips.

"You're going to get drenched," she said, recovering herself.

"Well what would you recommend?" Kenneth asked sarcastically. "That we call in a seamstress?"

"I'm sorry, Ken. Don't be like that. Look, how about if you each use another bag as a skirt? Here," she said, grabbing one from the roll and making a waist-sized opening in the bottom of it. She held it for Charles who stepped into it and with arms raised like a kid being fitted for his Halloween costume, let Jocelyn tuck it into the waistband of his trousers. Tom and Kenneth followed suit, and thus vested and skirted in plastic, their feet still encased in the white bags, the three men made for the door looking like transvestites on a cheap budget.

"I wish I had a camera," Jocelyn said, unable to keep from laughing. Charles curtsied for her.

"Too bad about the shoes though," Karenza said.

"What's wrong with them?" Tom asked, pointing one of his like a ballerina.

"You're not supposed to wear white after September," she said.

"Oh, how gauche of us," Kenneth said, and headed out the door, flashlight in hand, and Tom and Charles colliding with each other as they followed.

"God help us," Jocelyn said, as the door shut behind them.

Sarah, eyes still closed, whimpered from the window seat.

Karenza looked from Sarah to the fireplace, "We don't want

this to go out, you know," she rubbed her arms to warm up a bit. "Depending on which direction the wind is coming from the wood out there could be quite wet."

"Well, what can we use to keep it going?" she nodded at the nearly flameless grate.

"I don't know. The furniture?"

"Not a bad idea," Jocelyn laughed. "I was never big on chintz. But your boss may not appreciate that. What about some of these cheap paperbacks?"

"Ew," Karenza winced. "That's a bit too *Fahrenheit 451* for me."

"Oh come on Karenza, look at this so-called library. It's hardly a monument to the intellect, is it?"

"Oh, all right," Karenza conceded. "But make sure you start with the crappy ones. I'll go and get some blankets."

"Good plan."

Karenza stopped at the door and turning back to Jocelyn said, "I had you all wrong," and was gone before Jocelyn could fulfill the urge to hug her. Instead, she turned her attention to the book-case and with the aid of a candle, began searching its shelves for the initial sacrifice, giggling as she reached for a paperback edition of *Bonfire of the Vanities*.

The inn had only six bedrooms upstairs, each with en suite bath-rooms. Karenza did the rounds collecting blankets as she went, and then inevitably found herself in Tom's room. He'd been given the room directly over the lounge, as she would have supposed. It was the best room after all, facing the sea. But rain had been driven in by the wind, and found its way through the leaky sill, a small puddle already gathering on the floor below the window. Not wanting to use one of Tom's towels as a sop, she returned to another bathroom to retrieve enough not only to place on the floor and at the sill, but for drying off the men on their return from wood gathering.

She took a moment to check out his toiletries, not surprised to find them neatly lined up on the shelf below the mirror, all of them exuding quiet luxury: the olive wood toothbrush, the Braun electric shaver, and a bottle of Armani Eau Pour Homme. She unscrewed the cap and wafting the bottle under her nose, recognized the smell of him from when she'd stood behind him in the kitchen, her face having grazed his neck as she'd squeezed his penis. She liked its woody spiciness and splashed a little behind her ears and into the hair at the nape of her neck, which she knew would retain the aroma longer than would her skin. His toiletry bag sat on the stand next to the sink, a plain zipped bag of soft black leather. Looking inside, she saw dental floss, a nail clipper and several lambskin condoms two of which she slipped into the back pocket of her jeans and then, unzipping her jeans, helped herself to a little more cologne, which she patted into the crotch of her knickers.

This bedroom was her favourite in the inn, not only because of the view, but also because of the four-poster bed. She sat down on it for a moment, and flashed the torch around the room. The latest in Samsonite wheeled luggage, neatly placed on the suitcase rack, which on inspection she saw held a couple of bespoke shirts, a grey cashmere crewneck sweater, and some clean underwear and socks. A separate zipped insert held the shirt and underwear he must have worn that day. His Hugo Boss suit hung in the wardrobe with a pair of neatly placed, Chelsea-style boots, handmade in Italy and a black corduroy jacket.

On the desk in front of the window, carefully lined up like the precious objects they were, sat a PowerBook G3, his Nokia mobile phone and a tiny leather book that on closer inspection turned out to be a Hermès address book. On the bedside table, a copy of Paul Krugman's *The Return of Depression Economics* lay open to a chapter entitled "Masters of the Universe: Hedge Funds and Other Villains."

Karenza lay on the bed and watched the rain's steady rush down the dark window through which the occasional green glow from the lighthouse on Godrevy Island bore all the comfort of a distant planet.

21

Charles, Tom and Kenneth stood under the eaves outside the kitchen, waiting for their eyes to adjust to a black on black landscape. In comparison, the candlelit lounge now seemed like a fully lit stage set. And it wasn't just the darkness that had the men huddled together in silence; the cacophony of the wind as it dervished through trees and bushes that creaked and groaned suggested there was more damage to come. Yet even these sounds diminished in intensity when compared to that of the sea's relentless crash against the base of the cliff, the edge of which disappeared some fifty feet to the right of where the men stood watching the waves race landward like white panthers.

Charles and Tom, keepers of the flame so to speak, shone their torches in an arc, the beams sweeping across the car park, which was now awash with mud. At the far end they could see a lean-to, housing an impressive supply of wood.

Kenneth was the first to speak; his words, ripped from his mouth by the wind, were indecipherable by the end of the first sentence.

"What?" Tom yelled.

Kenneth cupped his torch-free hands to his mouth, "I said, I think we should find the damaged power line first. We don't want to get electrocuted!"

"OK!" Charles yelled. "But the tree crashed on the other side of the building, outside the lounge."

"So?"

"I don't think we have to worry about stepping on a live line."

"So what's the plan then?" Tom yelled.

Kenneth suggested they leave one torch hanging from the kitchen door to illuminate their return, and use the other to make their way to the woodpile and start carrying armfuls back inside. Glad to be in command, Kenneth stepped off the doorstep and immediately went arse-up, the plastic of his bagged feet gliding through the mud like a palette knife on icing. If it hadn't been so shocking, it would have been hilarious to see the other two instinctively go to his aid only to end up in the same position, the three of them then scrambling over each other in an attempt to get up, rather like pups still slick from birth, blindly heading for the teat.

Charles let out a hearty chuckle as he slithered into Tom, who muttered grumpily, pissed off about his clothes being ruined.

"Get a grip," he yelled. Charles laughed even more.

"I would if I could! We'll have to take these bin-liners off and hope for traction via honey and ground glass." The bags duly removed, the men helped each other to their feet and with the rain driving into their faces, continued on their mission.

The woodpile had miraculously stayed dry thanks to a generous overhang in the design of the roof. With Kenneth holding the torch, the other two began loading up with logs which they deposited inside the kitchen door. They had completed four round trips and were going for the final one when Charles, reaching for some kindling at the back of the pile, dislodged what turned out to be a pivotally placed log, which in turn let loose a dozen more logs onto his left hand trapping his fingers with their bone-crushing weight.

"Jesus Christ! Fuck!" he screamed and howled with the pain. The sound was so primal it raised the hairs on Kenneth's neck, yet in spite of its volume, it was no match for nature's Wagnerian opera and therefore went unheard by Tom who, having already reached the kitchen door, let himself in and headed toward the lounge with the first load of wood.

Having managed to rekindle the fire with the addition of some paperback romances and the contents of a tube of pick-up-sticks, Jocelyn continued to fan the flames with the magazine Charles had been reading. She prided herself on her fire-making ability and was reminded of the woodstove she'd lived with for eight years in upstate New York. Of course, she mused, at that point in her life she was drinking so heavily she could probably have revived a fire just by breathing on it.

She'd escaped Manhattan in nineteen eighty-four, tired of waitressing, tired of husbands, but not yet tired of alcohol. She'd taken Mimi, her then ten-year-old daughter, and done a geo-graphic, convinced that living a simple life, in a rural area, away from the relentlessly ambitious energy of the city, would solve all her problems. She'd received a small settlement from her lat-est divorce, which she figured, could last three years if she lived frugally. Maybe longer if her New York dealer continued to show and sell her work. Anyway, enough time to devote all her energy to painting.

If she'd drawn a graph of her life up to that point it would have shown ever-increasing highs and lows, the distance between each narrowing every year; the lower the fall, the higher the rebound and vice versa. She recognized now that all her decisions back then had been based on the latest trauma and were applied like Band-Aids slapped onto what cursorily appeared to be surface scrapes, the origins of which she was not conscious of any more than she was able to judge their severity.

This was how she had concluded they must move to New Paltz, some ninety miles north of Manhattan. Her latest affair had fizzled, and the city suddenly seemed overwhelming. Small town life, she convinced herself, would be the answer. New Paltz was the Band Aid at hand at the time. She chose it, sight unseen, based on the recommendation of a one-night stand with a twenty-one-year-old recently graduated from its college.

Her knack for recovery, albeit not yet in sobriety, was uncanny and she'd always managed to land on her feet. Within two days of arrival in the town, she'd secured the rental of a small cottage on a large estate. The owners, who occupied the main house, came up from the city on weekends. They offered Jocelyn the cottage free of rent in exchange for her keeping an eye on the place. Its obvious drawbacks, not obvious to Jocelyn at the time, included its remoteness from the village proper and its size; the downstairs housed an open-plan living-kitchen-dining area along with the only bedroom and bathroom. Upstairs consisted of a half-floor loft which doubled as Jocelyn's bedroom and studio in the winter. In the warmer months she used a small uninsulated barn as her studio.

The other major drawback was the sole method of heating; a cast iron woodstove whose chimney heated the upstairs before exiting the roof. She remembered what a disaster it had been that first night in the cottage. It had been almost dark by the time they arrived, having left the city late afternoon and then stopping at the local supermarket for provisions. It was mid-October; Indian summer had come and gone leaving behind crisp days and cold nights. She had forgotten to bring the house instructions and so had no idea how to turn on the water which had been turned off in order to protect the pipes against an early freeze. At least they had electricity and the fridge was running. How bad could it be, she'd cheerfully told Mimi, who was already familiar with the leaky boat of her mother's life.

After almost an hour of struggling to light the woodstove, only to be rewarded with a roomful of smoke, they had suppered on bread and cheese and then huddled in Mimi's bed under all available blankets. The only saving grace was that it being Sunday, she had been unable to buy booze and so was at least capable of waking on time to feed and drive Mimi to her new school. Before returning to the cottage she had stopped at the liquor store and then the hardware store where she dazzled one of the men into accompanying her home and teaching her how to operate the woodstove.

By the time she moved back to the city in '92 to begin teaching at the School of Visual Arts, she had sworn off alcohol and woodstoves. When she and Charles decided to live together they had both wanted an apartment with a fireplace but she had left the operating of it to Charles, loving the ease and efficiency of his manual dexterity. Now, as she felt the satisfaction of her own survival skills she wondered what other capabilities she might have relinquished in order to feel taken care of.

The door opened and there was Tom, draped in torn, mud-covered plastic holding an armful of wood with all the pride of a new father. He took a step toward Jocelyn.

"Don't move," she cried, looking at his feet. She removed three of the skinniest logs from his arms, arranged them in the grate, and then returned for the others, which she placed on the hearth.

"Look at the state of you! It must have been awful out there. Don't you think you ought to get those wet things off?" she added, suggesting he leave his clothes in the kitchen, where presumably there would be a machine for laundering table linens. Then she carefully removing the red chenille blanket from the still-unconscious Sarah, gave it to Tom, and invited him to get creative with his new wardrobe.

"Oh, that's OK, I have more clothes upstairs."

"Yeah but you can't traipse up there in that muddy stuff can you," She waved the blanket at him like a toreador. "I promise not to look," she said and started back to the fire, but almost immediately turned back to Tom. "Hey, where are Charles and Kenneth?"

"I'm not sure," he said. "Having a quiet smoke on the veranda, perhaps?"

22
....

"Oh, God, oh God," Charles chanted, as Kenneth began carefully and efficiently to remove the logs from his trapped hand, making sure not to dislodge more in the process. It was obvious to both men that as an oncology surgeon, Charles's hands were his income.

"I think I might have done some damage here," Charles said with foreboding. "We could be looking at fractures to the metacarpals. Please God, I hope not. Ooh, ah, easy, easy," he said, as Kenneth removed the last log.

"Come on old boy, let's get you inside," Kenneth said, holding Charles's right arm and guiding him towards the kitchen.

"Oh, God, oh, please, God." Charles's continued incantation of a deity whose existence he had strongly argued against so recently, would have struck him as ironic if it weren't for the pain. As they made their way into the house, Charles's mind flooded with thoughts as the scenario unfolded before him. At fifty-two, he had, he felt, another fifteen, twenty years of practice ahead of him. Apart from deepening his relationship with Jocelyn and traveling, he had yet to consider how he'd like to fill his time after retirement. A hobbyist he was not. He enjoyed swimming and tennis, the former for its meditative quality and the latter for its collaborative competition, but he wouldn't call them passions. Did he have passions? As the throbbing in his hand increased, along with his awareness of how this injury might affect his career, he realized that his career was not a passion; it was his identity. If he lost his career, did he lose his identity? If so, how could he ever hope to find passion? The sexual passion that he and Jocelyn still shared with intensity if with less frequency, had nothing to do with self-fulfillment, but was merely a momentary self-abandonment of the definitive, "I am" that fleetingly allowed for the split second unity of "we are," and was, he knew, hardly enough to fill the future, which suddenly seemed as howlingly vast as the sea.

Karenza had made several journeys down the stairs carrying her haul of blankets and towels. Making a final journey along the hallway with torch and kettle, she startled Kenneth and Charles as they made their way to the lounge. Kenneth's torch swung wildly, its beam momentarily lighting her up as hers illuminated them.

"What's going on?" she asked, lowering the torch and in the process saw the two men like clay sculptures, the mud sliding off their partially ripped plastic gear. And then she saw Charles's hand. "Oh my God," she gasped. "What have you done?" She set down the load she was carrying on the reception desk and shone her torch directly at Charles's swollen and battered hand. "Ooh that looks nasty, you must be in shock. You'd better sit down. Look, over here," she shone the torch to one of the leather armchairs that furnished the vestibule. "Then you need to get those wet clothes off."

"Thanks, Karenza," said Charles, sounding grateful for her practical approach. Kenneth laid his torch on the reception desk so as to more easily support Charles, who seemed close to faint-ing, and carefully lowered him into the chair.

Having handed them both towels from her supply, Karenza began easing the plastic bags off Charles, being careful to avoid bashing his injured hand while Kenneth mumbled something about having to strip off in public. "And when you've finished wrap yourself in this and help Charles undress. Here's a blanket for him. I'm going to get ice." Charles, once again grateful for her capability, asked her if she could also find scissors and some clean cloth.

Kenneth, draped in lilac candlewick, held the lounge door open for Charles, who was now clad in tartan wool. The entrance of the two men triggered hysterical laughter from Tom and Jocelyn until she saw the blood.

"Oh my God," she cried.

Kenneth looked over at Sarah, still comatose on the window seat and felt gratitude that the word of God had not revived her.

"I need alcohol," Charles said.

"Don't we all," Tom muttered.

"Not to drink, you fool. I need to sterilize my hand."

"What the hell happened?" Tom asked.

Kenneth filled him in while Jocelyn, who was already reaching for the brandy, called over her shoulder to Tom, "Put him on the couch, feet up. Keep your arm up, darling, I'll be right there."

Charles's thumb had escaped injury, but the ends of all four fingers were smashed and bleeding as was the skin on the back of his hand.

Karenza returned with ice, a clean tea towel and scissors. She'd also managed to find gauze and Ibuprofen in the kitchen's inadequately stocked first-aid kit. Jocelyn went to work, following Charles's instructions, first handing him a shot of brandy to drink and then dabbing vodka onto the abrasions, an application that shriveled his testicles and had him beseeching God once again. The hand, duly bandaged with gauze and a strip of tea towel, on top of which an ice pack was placed, was then laid to rest on a cushion.

Karenza looked around the room; the fire was merry in its grate having dined on literature and pulp fiction before moving onto the main course of freshly gathered wood. Candlelight glowed, softening fabrics if not faces. The kettle, balanced nicely on the grate, began to sing its age-old song. Was it imagination, or had the wind died down a little? Tom and Kenneth, sitting cross-legged on the floor in front of the fire could have been robed tribesmen. Sarah, continued her light snore. Jocelyn had pulled a chair over next to Charles and was holding his good hand and stroking his head. It felt to Karenza as if they were a tableau, frozen in position for eternity.

"So," she said. "How do we all feel about impermanence now?"

23

....

The Ibuprofen, having taken the edge off the pain, and the brandy—Charles not being a hard liquor man—if not warming the cockles of his heart then at least redirecting the neurons in his brain, allowed him the chance to ponder an answer to Karenza's question.

"Actually," he said, "I feel a lot better about the impermanence idea than I do about my original one."

"Ooh, you cheated," Karenza teased.

"Not really. I reconsidered."

"Well, what *were* you going to say?" Jocelyn asked, slightly peeved that she might have been put through the ringer unnecessarily.

"Entropy."

As he had anticipated he was greeted with silence. It was one of those words: either you knew what it meant, or you didn't. It was Jocelyn who had the courage to ask, but Karenza, like an eager schoolchild, interjected immediately.

"Doesn't it mean everything eventually falls apart?"

"Isn't that a bit like impermanence," said Jocelyn, glumly.

"No, not really. Karenza's close," Charles said. "It's original definition was very specific, but it's also used figuratively to describe the deterioration of a system or society. Or it can just mean a state of chaos, disorganization and randomness."

"Well," Kenneth said. "We have certainly seen all of that in action tonight, haven't we?"

"Either way," Jocelyn said, feeling discomforted by Charles again. "They're not very positive beliefs, are they? What's 'entropy' got to do with 'the thing we most believe in for the new millennium'? Isn't that what the game's supposed to be about? Surely, you don't want chaos. I mean, if we all believed in those things we'd give up, wouldn't we. Who would be bothered doing anything if all you believed in was chaos and randomness, never mind that everything ends." The emotion in Jocelyn's voice was now audible.

"I didn't say that's all I believe in," Charles said quietly. "I believe in lots of things, but not all of them are provable. I thought we were supposed to put forward the thing we most believe in. I took that to mean that it would have to be an absolute, irrefutable fact. God is obviously refutable, and as far as the majority of us here are concerned, totally not based in fact." Charles appealed to Jocelyn. "It's only a game, after all."

Silence fell again, before Kenneth said, "Well, I think entropy and impermanence are inarguable, but like Jocelyn, I do find them rather bleak. Funny how we all invoke God when we're pain though," Kenneth added, mindful of Charles's recent incantations.

"Oh, come on," Karenza said, "*God* is an expletive, not a religion. I'm much more interested in this impermanence idea— especially as Charles may have done *permanent* damage to his hand."

"She's got a point," Charles admitted. "And I can tell you right now that when you're in pain you are convinced it's going to be that way forever. Hopefully I haven't done *permanent* damage to my hand and the pain will go away. Then I can remember this experience and maybe have more compassion for my patients."

"But you always say that the memory of pain is impermanent," Jocelyn said.

"Once the pain has gone, yes. Like after childbirth . . ."

"Depends what kind of pain you're talking about," Karenza interrupted. Karenza, the archer. Karenza, with the unerring instinct for the bull's eye of the psychic wounds of others; Karenza who used this instinct to deflect the arrow's re-entry into the center of her own pain. "What about psychological pain? That lasts forever." And her flint-tipped arrow struck them all in the same moment, the quiver of history felt by each and every one of them. But unexpectedly, it was Charles who appeared to feel the full force of the arrow's thrust. With a startled look on his face he at first tried to respond to her, but for all his articulacy up to now, he seemed confused and unable to produce any words. Then an involuntary sound escaped from him the sound torn out of him much as had been his earlier howl of physical pain.

"Darling," Jocelyn said, leaning over him, "what is it?" He let his head drop back onto the sofa's arm as if in resignation, his eyes squeezed shut as his body began to shake. Jocelyn, by now kneeling on the ground next to him, was kissing his good hand fervently. "What is it? My darling, what's the matter?"

He continued to sob, silently.

"Sweetheart, tell me what's happening."

"I can't." He started pulling at his collar with his good hand as though he was suffocating.

Jocelyn, stroked his forehead, "It's all right, Charles, I'm here."

"Yes, but he's not," Charles's voice cracked.

"Who?

"Dad. Dad's not here. He'll never be here . . . and it's my fault."

"Darling, what are you saying?"

"He killed himself," he sobbed, giving his body in to the release of long-repressed emotion. "I thought he'd always be there for me. He was the one permanent thing in my life and he killed himself." Charles turned his face to Jocelyn, who mopped the tears rolling down his cheeks. "I broke his heart and he killed himself."

"What do you mean, darling? What could you possibly have done to break his heart? He must have been so proud of you." Jocelyn was struggling to understand where all this had come from.

"He built that business from scratch. He was clever. He found a niche. He was successful."

"What did he do?" Karenza didn't appear to want to let up with the steely questioning and dragged a chair closer to the sofa.

"He was a jeweler. He opened a small shop off Madison Avenue selling engagement rings—all his designs. It took off because they were affordable, postwar, when love was in the air." Charles, still sniffing, took the handkerchief from Jocelyn in an attempt to regain his composure. "Anway, he taught me how to polish stones, file the settings, all that stuff. So that I could take the business over sometime and I guess I was never clear with him that I didn't want that. I just let him continue to believe."

"So, what? You just didn't like the work?" asked Karenza.

"No, not that completely. I liked the precision work. Guess that's why I ended up as a surgeon."

"But darling, you don't know for sure that deciding not to go into the business was the reason for him . . . well, was the cause of . . ." Jocelyn was trying to find the right words.

"But I do. That's the thing. I finally told him after I finished at Harvard. He wept, Jocelyn, right there in front of me. And then a week later he hanged himself."

Charles blew his nose and then in barely a whisper said, "Do you know the worst thing? I really wanted to be a psychiatrist. I let go of that dream to become a surgeon under pressure from my first wife, but I didn't even consider compromising for Dad. Now that's really shit."

"What an agony that must have been for you," Kenneth said.

"It was," Charles admitted. Unable to make eye contact with anyone, he stared at the fire.

"What kept you going?" Tom asked.

"I don't know really. I think I just tried to stick to the plan. I'd made this decision, and now I had to make it work."

"So you didn't believe in entropy back then?" Karenza said.

"Meaning . . . ?" Tom asked somewhat sharply.

"Meaning entropy doesn't equate with thinking that sticking to a plan will make order out of chaos." The hint of sarcasm in Karenza's tone did not go unmissed.

"No, I didn't think about things like entropy back then. Too busy trying to protect myself," Charles said, giving Jocelyn's arm a light squeeze. Tom chucked a couple more logs on the fire and gave them a good poke. The blaze was doing a good job so far. A towel had been rolled up and placed along the bottom of the door to keep heat from escaping and the room was maintaining its heat. It was agreed that the wood still left in the kitchen would last a good few hours before anyone had to brave the elements again.

"Why have you never told me this?" Jocelyn asked.

"The same reason you never told me your family secret I guess; a mixture of guilt and shame and fear. Not to mention denial. It's as though if something is never uttered out loud then we can pretend it never actually happened. Of course, that's bullshit."

There was silence for a while, as each of them ruminated on the validity of what Charles had said.

"But can we just go back a bit?" Tom asked. "If you believe in all this impermanence and entropy stuff and therefore that things don't happen for a reason, how the hell do you manage to be such a generally cheerful person?"

"I've no idea," Charles said. "It's just my nature I suppose."

"Oh, that's a bit lame," said Karenza flicking an ember off the carpet back into the grate.

"That's not fair," Jocelyn was beginning to rally. "He's just saying you can choose how to react to a random act befalling you. But hey, don't think I'm agreeing with you, Charles." Jocelyn said giving him a wry smile.

"I'm not following," Karenza said.

"Me neither," said Tom.

"Okay, here's a couple of examples right here. Kenneth and I, and Charles, had fathers who committed acts that had nothing to do with us. But look at the impact on our lives and look what we did with it. I was the *consequence* of my father's behaviour, not the reason for it any more than Kenneth was. Charles's dad's suicide didn't happen to Charles for a *reason*. And Charles wasn't the reason for his father's suicide. But Charles was young when it happened, as was Kenneth when he saw what he saw, barely adults, either of them, and so they became victims of those acts. But as adults we have the option to make different decisions, reasoned ones. Deciding not to be a victim is the exact opposite of randomness. But it still doesn't mean that the shitty thing that happened, happened so that we could make a good decision. Am I making any sense!"

She paused for a moment and the looks of confusion that greeted her caused her to retreat a little. "I'm sorry," she said. "I'm not really expressing myself well. I've never really verbalized these thoughts before and they obviously need more consideration."

"No, no," Charles said. "I think you did a pretty good job, actually." He went to reach for her with his wounded hand and gasped as the pain flared.

"Oh, darling, what can I do for you?" she asked, stroking his brow.

"Just what you're doing," he said.

"So, let me see if I have this right," Karenza said. "What Jocelyn is saying is that your injury didn't happen for a reason, but the fact that it did happen gives you the opportunity to decide what to do as a result?"

"Perfectly put," Jocelyn said.

"Any ideas yet?" Karenza asked Charles.

"More Ibuprofen, more ice, a wee bit more brandy and when we get out of here, some good medical attention."

"And if there is permanent damage to your hand?" Karenza persisted.

"Then my career as a surgeon will become yet another example of impermanence. How about that? Pretty neat, huh?"

Sarah let out a snore that sounded more like a guffaw, its explosion jolting her upright, the sudden movement sending the room spinning. She looked around the lounge taking in the men clad in their assorted bedcovers and wondered if it was something she ate.

"Did I miss something?" she asked.

Kenneth wanted to tell her she *was* the missing something, instead he said, "impermanence," omitting the word entropy probably because he was sure she didn't know what it meant and old habits being what they are, still had the need to rescue her from embarrassment.

Jocelyn, seeing how disoriented her sister-in-law was, whispered an explanation of what had been happening while she had been asleep.

Sarah stared at her, unblinking. "Are you serious?" she asked, when Jocelyn finished. "Three men who were formally attired in plastic bags are now wearing bedspreads and one of them has obviously sustained an injury and now you're telling me it's all something to do with chaos?"

"For God's sake, Sarah," Kenneth said.

"Oh, Him again," she said and with her right foot, hooked the bottom shelf of the wheeled drinks trolley and pulled it towards her. "Drinkies, anyone?" she asked, already reaching for the brandy decanter.

Tom looked horrified and repulsed. "Don't you think maybe you should have a coffee instead?" his voice spikier than he was expecting.

"Oh, aren't you the goody-goody," she said, taking a sip from her refilled teacup. "Good stuff this," she said, swinging her feet like a little girl. "It's what they put in the doggie's barrel when they send him out on a rescue mission. Looks like no one sent the doggie out for you lot," she giggled. Kenneth's clenched fists and rigid jaw said it all.

Karenza poured more water into the kettle offering to make tea once it had boiled. Sarah took a hearty slug of her brandy. "Must have been frightening that a retired army officer, a surgeon, and a buff young lawyer can be so easily clobbered by nature. Hah!" Sarah chortled at her own joke.

Karenza giggled. Sarah's unpredictability unsettled her but she also enjoyed these intermittent gems when the woman told it like it was.

Jocelyn shot a look at Sarah. Just moments ago their little group had seemed to have let down its individual defenses and, dare she say, were actually showing concern for one another, only to be stirred up again by a drunk. Flashes of her own boozy behavior and the ways in which, once drunk, she became a shit-stirrer, didn't stop her from lashing out at Sarah.

"What right do you have to be so scathing?" she yelled. "Where were you when we were all doing our best to cope with an emergency? Sleeping off your last round of drinks while everyone else went to work."

"Oh, get you Ada," Sarah said. "The reformed alcoholic who now can do no wrong. You weren't so good at coming to the rescue when I lost my babies, were you?"

"Oh, please," Charles begged. "Can we please move on."

"What's the matter Charlie," Sarah prodded. "Is your wittle hand hurting?"

"Hurting!" Tom yelled, "You ridiculous woman. You've been snoring off the booze and now you're making fun of him? What's the matter with you?"

"Oh, take it easy, dear. He's a big boy, aren't you, Charlie? He'll get it sorted. He's from America. They've got the biggest and best of everything." She took another sip of brandy. "But, I agree, time to move on," she reached for the vase, which had been left on the trolley after the last draw. She held it out to Charles.

"Your turn, I believe."

"No. I've had my turn."

"How quickly you forget," said Kenneth.

"Oh, shut up."

"For Christ's sake, give it to me," Karenza said, walking over to Sarah and taking the vase. She reached in, pulled out the next piece of paper and burst out laughing.

"What's so funny?" Sarah asked.

"It says, wait for it . . . 'Civility'!"

> PART III <

24

"That's mine," Kenneth said, coughing self-consciously in antici-pation of the onslaught.

"Oh, what a surprise," said Sarah.

"What's more of a surprise," he hissed, turning to her. "Is that after being married to *you* for thirty years, I still believe in it."

The wind had picked up again, as if to compete with the agi-tation in the lounge. A puff of smoke backed into the room from the fireplace. Kenneth immediately went to work banking the logs to the back of the grate directing the flames farther up the chimney and thereby eliminating the backdraft.

"I hate to say this, but we should probably open the door a crack," he said. "What do you think?" he asked the group.

"Well, the *civil* thing to do would be to take a vote," Charles quipped, bringing a little good humour back to the room. The vote was unanimously in favour with one abstention on the part of Sarah. Tom removed the rolled towel and opened the door, the cold air immediately sucking out the smoke along with some of the heat.

Together they moved the couch and chairs closer to the fire and piled on some more blankets. And so the little group grew closer, except for Sarah, who, further entrenching her position as the outsider, remained on the window seat from where she had the choice of looking out the window to the bleak world beyond, or staring at the backs of the other five. It was anyone's guess how much of her self-imposed exile was to do with the unobservable access she had to the trolley.

Karenza poured the now boiling water into the teapot and Tom broke open a package of digestive biscuits.

"So come on, Kenneth. Go for it!" Karenza urged.

Hesitating a little, he began. "Well, it may seem a little soft, but in the new millennium, we would do well to remember that a little civility goes a long way. Courteous behavior. Respect for others. Decorum in public places. Unfortunately, it's gone out of fashion."

"And why is it so important to you?" Charles asked.

"Well, without it we're one step away from being barbarians. The Internet and mobile phones are beginning to eat away at basic social skills and we need to think about where this is going to take us, don't you agree?"

"Yes, but it's a bit idealistic, isn't it?" Tom said. "I mean, in a perfect world, okay, yes, that's great. But we don't live in a civil world. It's not just about new technology. Look at Rwanda, look at the Serbo-Croatian war. Not much civility going on there. Not to mention how well Israel and the Palestinians are doing on that front."

"I'm afraid Tom is right," Charles said, "You can't make people act civilly anymore than you can export democracy."

"So, what are you suggesting?" Kenneth asked. "That because not everyone is capable or willing to be civil that we should just chuck it?'

"No," Jocelyn interjected. "I'm with you, Kenneth. Those of us who are capable of it should most definitely practice it. It makes me think of that parable of the little boy walking along the shore. The tide has stranded thousands of starfish and he starts putting them back in the sea. An old man coming in the other direction asks him what's the use of that, you can't save them all, and the little boy says, but if I can save even one it's worth it."

"Well excuse my *in*civility." Karenza was back with a vengeance. "But I think you're all talking bollocks. I think 'civility,' " she mimed the speech marks around the word, "is close to extinction and rightly so. It's one of those phony acts people do when someone's looking, but behind closed doors it's a whole other story."

"What do you mean?" Kenneth asked.

"Well, look how many men put on a show of holding a door open for a woman and an hour later the same guy is beating the shit out of his wife."

"Look," Kenneth said, "I'm not saying that there aren't some people for whom it's a sham. Obviously. But I believe in its worth and I believe we should fight for it."

"Oh, listen to you," Sarah said from her perch on the window seat. "The soldier who never went into battle believes there's something worth fighting for."

"Well, there's a charming example of someone being civil," Kenneth said. He'd become somewhat inured to his wife's passive aggressive observations, but he'd never heard her as openly hostile as she was tonight.

"Oh, for Chrissake," Sarah said. "You've used your kind of fake courtesy as a cover up ever since I've known you."

"A cover up for what, might I ask?"

"For your anger and cowardice."

"Whoa!" Karenza exclaimed. Even she was feeling a bit disconcerted by Sarah's tone.

"You can talk," Kenneth said. "At least I did something meaningful with my life. I didn't sit at home watching TV and boozing the night away while I thought no one was looking."

"Well, you certainly never looked, did you? Even before I started drinking you never looked. Oh, but you were always very civil," she sneered. "I could have been anyone. Even when you fucked me you never looked at me. Not that you did that very often. Fucking wouldn't exactly be considered a civil act for you, would it?"

Enraged, Kenneth stood up, the furniture fortunately blocking easy access to his wife. "You know what?" he said, "Fuck you and fuck civility! I've changed my mind. You're right, Karenza, civility is bollocks. I've tried to live by it for the last forty-five years. I never told anyone that I knew what my father had done ... I thought by keeping up appearances we could all pretend nothing had really happened. I thought Jocelyn could grow up and live her life without the pain of knowing the truth. But you know what? The pain of truth is nothing compared to the pain of keeping a secret." He slumped back down in his chair, exhausted. "You're right, Sarah, I have been a coward. I was a coward as a soldier and a coward as a civilian. And lord knows, I've been a coward as a husband. But then I don't think either of us has ever told the truth. If we had we wouldn't be where we are now."

"And where is that?" Sarah asked. "Besides being stranded at the edge of a cliff." She started weaving her way to the door.

"That's right," Kenneth yelled. "Walk away. You'd think a vicar's daughter might be interested in truth, but you're so far from it you actually pretend that you believe in God. It's a good job your father's lost his memory. If he knew how hypocritical his daughter is, he'd be mortified."

Sarah had reached the door, the handle of which she now clung to as she turned to look at Kenneth. "My father, mortified? Hypocrisy? He was the epitome of hypocrisy. My father? Preaching civility every Sunday and getting blowjobs from the choirboys during the week. Your father was a bastard. Mine was a pervert. How do you like that bit of truth?" she said, before slamming the door behind her.

To say the room went silent would be an understatement. What made the silence almost unbearable was the sudden absence of wind, as though the violence of history and tragedy had extinguished its breath leaving only the sound of rain; a sound so mournful it was as if nature was wringing its hands in anguish.

Kenneth, standing now, looked as though he'd been drained of blood. Jocelyn, struggling with tears, went to him and gently eased him back in his chair.

Tom, visibly shaken, wished he could escape upstairs and change into his suit trousers, but felt that such an act would be unkind given that Charles and Kenneth had no choice but to remain skirted.

"Karenza," Charles said almost apologetically. "Is there more Ibuprofen and ice?"

"Oh, yes. Of course." For the first time that evening Karenza was subdued.

"I think I should go check on Sarah," Jocelyn said, even though she dreaded what she might find. As she closed the door behind her the grandfather clocked chimed midnight, but not for a minute did any of them consider it was the beginning of a new day.

25

....

Sarah had a vague memory of a toilet near the bar and thought she might just be able to make it there. She hoped that once there, whatever was left of her insides could be flushed away just as all her babies had been. She'd never actually asked what happened to them. She had assumed that the four-month old fetuses were disposed of along with the gauze and latex gloves. But what happened to the stillborn? It was different these days. Now you were allowed to grieve for your stillborn child. You could even hold it, christen it, have a funeral for it, and bury it. But back then, in the early '70s a child carried to term but failing to breathe on entry was considered . . . what? A nonentity? A has-been that never was? There were no groups to join then, no sharing of common experience. Bereavement of a stillborn was a hushed affair. At least the hospital had the decency not to put her in the maternity ward after delivery. Nonetheless, she had heard the cries of the newborns as they wheeled her down the corridor. And who knew that the cry of someone else's baby would cause her milk to let down? Her body still holding that feeling of readiness despite having destroyed the thing she most wanted and was ready to hold in her arms: a child finally carried to term after three miscarriages. The near joy of the first contraction, the pain heralding the new arrival, was countered so soon after with the arrival dead on delivery. And then what? What had they done with her? She knew within an hour of arriving at the hospital that she was dead. They told her there was no heartbeat. The labour was induced to get her over and done with as quickly as possible: the horrendous, callous pain of induced labour, nonstop contractions for four hours. Four hours of pain at the centre of which was the knowledge that she still had to give birth. This agony had radiated from her innards and from her mind, which she was sure was no longer her own. Husbands not allowed in. Husbands saved from witnessing the passage of sorrow in its tiny blue-gray pallor. The husband, only that; a spouse but not a parent, shown in after all was clean and tidy, the baby and Sarah's uterus nonexistent. His face ashen, his shoulders usually squared to attention now rounded in inadequacy. The patted hand and there, there. She took every prescription they gave her, the sleeping pills, the pain pills, the Valium, the pills to dry up her milk. Kenneth took her home three days later, her small suitcase already packed when he arrived. She sat on the edge of the bed as if waiting to be picked up from a boarding school from which she had been expelled; failure, the only word on her report card. Then followed the silent drive home, the stop at the pet shop where she chose the runt of a litter of kittens to whom she gave the name of the dead baby. It was always a dead baby, never a daughter. The kitten, frail and fearful, submitted to Sarah's ministrations, the mismatched scale of which made the loss of the child even more unbearable. She asked Kenneth to return it to the pet shop the next day, an act for which she never forgave herself, while he struggled with feelings of grief and relief.

Sarah stumbled towards the bar, battled a wave of nausea and groping in the dark for a stool sat on it and waited for the bottles of spirits to come into focus.

When Jocelyn found her, Sarah was on the floor. There was a strong smell of urine. She went to her, knelt beside her, checked her pulse and finding it, pulled her into a sitting position and gently rocked her in her arms. "Sarah, Sarah, wake-up." Sarah's head lolled against Jocelyn's chest and then she looked up, searching Jocelyn's face in the dark.

"I think my waters have broken," she said.

26

Tom had put the last of the logs on the fire. The flames, having fed on the wickedness of words, gleefully licked their way up the chimney. He checked his watch and was disheartened to see that it was only half past midnight. "I should go and get some of the wood we left in the kitchen," he said.

"Better wait a while," Charles suggested. "We don't know where Jocelyn and Sarah are and you don't want to interrupt them right now."

"You're right," Tom agreed.

"Do you think I should go and help Jocelyn?" Karenza asked Charles, a gesture of kindness that surprised her almost as much as it surprised him.

"No yet," he said. "Let's wait a few minutes." He turned to Kenneth, "How are you feeling?"

Kenneth turned to him, a look of utter defenselessness on his face, "How am I feeling?" he repeated. "I don't really know. But I'm not feeling how I would have expected to feel under these circumstances. I suppose I feel burnt. But not to a crisp. More like the fire went through me instead of eating me up."

"The cleansing heat of truth," Charles murmured.

"Yes, something like that," Kenneth nodded. "Ironic, isn't it? To have lived one's life hiding behind a mask. Can't believe I came up with all that 'civility' crap. Do you think we're all afraid of the truth?" he asked, his question sounding more like a plea.

"Of course we are," Charles said. "Truth hurts."

"Yeah," Karenza said, reverting to her more familiar style, "and we all know men will do anything to avoid pain."

"And do you really believe women are any different?" Tom wasn't in the mood to let that one lie.

"Actually, yes," she said, "I think women have a greater capacity for pain and therefore a greater capacity for truth."

"Wow, it must be amazing to be you," Tom said.

Karenza grinned. "Anyway Kenneth, now you've dumped civility for truth how do you feel about the latest revelations?" Kenneth looked at her. She really was astounding. But not only would she probably get even closer to the truth, but, he sensed, she would somehow feel empowered by it. He was suddenly eager to find out what *she* believed in.

"You know, it's funny," he said. "I don't ever remember being asked how I felt in my whole life and now two of you are asking. It never rains but it pours, eh?"

"Since we're in truth mode I actually feel relieved but also a bit sad, and well, a bit frightened."

"What do you mean, relieved?" Tom asked.

"Well, it's all out in the open now isn't it, between Sarah and me, I mean. There's nothing left to protect. I feel like I don't have to soldier on anymore." He wondered now if he had chosen to be in military intelligence because it was a legitimate way of living with secrecy, of mastering it even. Another act of cowardice, he thought, choosing to focus on the nature of global-political secrecy in order to avoid shining a light on his own.

"And what about the sad bit?" Karenza asked, "What are you sad about?"

Kenneth looked at her for a moment. "Do you really have to ask?" he said, "I'm sad because I've wasted my life. I'm sad because my wife and I kept huge secrets from each other. I didn't know about her father. She never told me before what she just said."

"But she's drunk, "Karenza said. "How do you know she's telling the truth?"

"For God's sake Karenza, give it a rest," Tom said. "Who on earth would want to make up a story like that about their father?"

Karenza shrugged.

Kenneth turned to her and said, "You don't do sadness very well do you? It's new to me, too. Really feeling it I mean. Even as I'm saying this I'm pushing it away." He flicked at a loose thread of chenille and without looking up continued. "I'm afraid that if I felt all the sadness that's waiting for me, I'd die. Sarah and I have spent thirty years not exactly lying to each other, but not telling the truth either. How sad is that? How sad is it that we both had fathers who damaged us and yet we couldn't share that with each other and maybe be a source of comfort to each other?" A single tear rolled down his cheek. "How sad is it that the only way my wife can survive her pain is by getting drunk and lashing out? How sad is it that I never stood up to my father? That I never found the courage to tell anyone, ever, least of all myself, how I felt about anything? How very fucking British. How very fucking civil."

"Don't be too hard on yourself, Kenneth," Charles said. "Anyway, you shouldn't junk civility. True civility is important. It's about respecting others, whether it's on the street, in business, or in politics."

"Well, good luck there," Karenza said. "Anyone for tea?"

While she poured, Tom put more digestives on a plate and broke open a bar of the cooking chocolate. "The night has just begun," he said, and passed the plate around.

After a period of silence, Tom broke in. "Kenneth, you know you mentioned that you were feeling frightened? Do you mind if I ask you what you are frightened of?"

"That's probably the most civilly asked question of the evening," Kenneth laughed. "What am I frightened of? That my marriage is over for one thing. Even though it's been a bit of a sham, it's familiar. And that alone is frightening, to have to admit that

I'm so cowardly that I'd settle for the familiar over the truth." He turned his attention back to the loose thread, trying to push it back into the weave. "And I suppose I'm frightened about what to do next. I'm sixty-five years old. Is there still time to change? And Sarah? What about her? I wish I could help her, but I don't know how. What if I can't? What if I still keep trying to rescue her?" He let go of the errant thread and brushed another tear away. "What if I choose to forget everything that's happened here, and it becomes just another secret and life will be business as usual? What then?"

27

....

"Oh, Sarah, Sarah," Jocelyn said, rocking her sister-in-law in her arms. Even though it was dark she could sense the confusion on her face, the look of innocent joy fading as Sarah realized that the wetness she felt was urine, not amniotic fluid.

"I'm going to be sick," she said, panicking. Jocelyn dislodged herself and felt around the bar for something knowing there was no way she'd get Sarah to the toilet in time. She made out what looked like a bowl of lemons and emptying them in the sink made it back to Sarah just in time to catch a fragrant mix of roast beef, two veg, gravy, trifle, and cheese on toast, all marinated in close to a bottle of brandy.

Jocelyn detested vomit. She'd prided herself on being able to hold her booze, preferring to pass out before arriving at the stage where her stomach might rebel. She hadn't been that keen on Mimi's vomit either once she passed the spit-up stage of infancy. But this stuff, gushing out of Sarah, was *Exorcist* material, she thought, as she held her breath along with Sarah's head, praying that Sarah would stop before it reached splash level.

"Okay, okay," Sarah gasped. "Okay, I think I've finished."

"You think, or you are?"

"Yes, finished. Oh, God."

Now what, Jocelyn wondered, holding the bowl away from her and breathing through her mouth? God, no fucking electricity, no water, no nothing. What was she supposed to do with the bowl? Fuck it. She put it back on the bar where it had formerly held lemons, covered it with a bar cloth and hoped she'd remember it before they eventually left the inn. If they ever left.

"Oh Sarah," she said. "Poor Sarah. I've been a lousy sister-in-law, haven't I?"

A great sob tore out of Sarah as Jocelyn held her again. She sobbed like a cliché, her body wracked, hardly able to get her breath, teeth chattering. She tried to say something but couldn't control her mouth. Snot and tears were all over her face, like a distressed infant.

"I just ... I just ... I just want to die ... oh please, just let me die."

"I know, I know," Jocelyn said, and she did. The last two years of her drinking she had wanted to die. In fact had thought she was dying. Had actually, one night toward the end, dragged herself to the bathroom mirror because she wanted to see what she looked like dying. She had looked at her reflection and known that she was killing herself, had been fascinated with the awesome knowledge that this was what she looked like choosing to kill herself, because, drunk as she was, she knew, in that moment, that it was her choice. She held out for another week and then, on the weekend, when Mimi went to stay with a friend, she cold-turkeyed, spent a day shivering in bed, and the next day had dragged her sorry arse off to AA. She could still remember how she had felt walking down the basement steps of the Methodist church; could remember, as she entered the room, feeling herself get smaller and smaller, surprised to feel not diminishment, but relief at no longer being larger than life. She had also been surprised at how many familiar faces were in the room. If she could have, she would have carried Sarah to a meeting right then.

"Oh, Sarah," she said. "What are we going to do?"

"Don't leave me, please don't leave me," Sarah began crying again.

"I'm not leaving you, I'm here, it's okay," Jocelyn said and resumed rocking Sarah, and all the while she was wondering how she was going to clean her up, whether she should go get Kenneth. Charles couldn't help, not with his hand like that. When Sarah had calmed down again, Jocelyn grabbed a cushion off the banquette and put it under her head.

"I'm going to get something to clean you up with and something for you to wear."

"No, oh no, please, don't leave me."

"Stop it, Sarah. I'll be right back."

"Don't bring anyone with you, promise me you won't bring anyone back with you?"

Jocelyn promised, but decided to go back to the lounge for help and ran in to Karenza in the reception area.

"We've got to stop meeting like this," she whispered.

"They don't call it reception for nothing," Karenza whispered back and the two of them started giggling.

"I came to see if I could help," Karenza said. "What's going on?"

Jocelyn filled her in.

"Ugh, I hate vomit," Karenza said.

"Me too," said Jocelyn and they started off again.

"Come on," Jocelyn said. "We've got to get it together. We need water and a cloth to start with."

"I've got the picture," said Karenza. "Leave it to me, you go back to Sarah and I'll be right there."

"She's not going to like your being there."

"Too bad," Karenza said, and headed for the kitchen.

Jocelyn went back to the bar room where Sarah had managed to drag herself onto the banquette. She was shivering.

"I wet myself," she whispered.

"I know. Karenza came to help, she's going to bring clean up supplies."

"Oh, no. You promised. How could you?" Sarah started to cry and then pulled herself together and lashed out at Jocelyn, "You're enjoying this aren't you? I bet it makes you feel really superior."

"For Christsake Sarah, shut the fuck up. You think I'm enjoying this? You think I don't know what you're going through? Believe me, I know. And I did more damage as a drunk than you could ever imagine. I'm not enjoying this. I'm finding it extremely painful. And I can't do anything about it. Just like no one could help me. I can't help you. I can clean you up, but I can't get you sober. You have to do that yourself and until you do you're always going to want to die."

Karenza came in. "Jackpot!" she cried, and then gagged. "Oh my God. . . . Where is it? I don't want to step in it."

"It's on the bar."

"On the bar! Are you fucking kidding me?"

"Don't worry, it's in the lemon bowl."

"Oh, nice. Put a paper umbrella it and call it a brandy sour."

Even Sarah laughed. And then they got busy. Karenza had brought a roll of paper towels from the kitchen and a bottle of fizzy water. Jocelyn washed Sarah's face and then soaked another wad of paper towel and gave it to Sarah. "You get to clean the nether regions," she said, helping Sarah get out of her knickers.

"My skirt is wet, too," Sarah said.

"I've got just the thing," Karenza said. "Get undressed," she ordered, and before Sarah could object, she held up a pair of handyman's overalls. Made of worn, blue, heavyweight cotton they looked more like a mechanic's outfit, long-sleeved and with a zip from crotch to collar. They were actually a pretty good fit.

"You'll look like Rosie the Riveter," Jocelyn said.

"Now let's get some hot tea and a digestive in you," Karenza said, turning to leave.

"Oh, I can't go back in there," Sarah said. "Please, I can't."

"Well we can't stay here, it's freezing," Jocelyn said.

"Oh, but I can't," Sarah began crying. "They'll all know."

"Know what?" Jocelyn asked.

"That I made a mess."

"You did that before you left the lounge," Karenza said sarcastically. "Let's go."

The three women held hands and with Sarah in the middle felt their way back to the rest of the group.

28

Tom hadn't seen a grown man weep since the night his father came back from identifying Tom's mother at the morgue. She'd been found in a bed-sit in Earl's Court. The landlord had gone there to claim the overdue rent, but when he got no response he had let himself in to leave the eviction notice on her table. She'd been dead a couple of days.

Tom and his father had neither seen nor heard from her for two years at that point. The landlord had called the police, but not before going through her handbag and suitcase in the hope of finding money. The search had yielded two pounds and some change. In her handbag was a new packet of cigarettes, some condoms, and a powder compact that had been a gift from Tom's father. There was also a photograph. A typical holiday snapshot of the three of them, taken on some promenade, the good-looking parents holding their two-year-old boy, nothing but good times ahead.

Tom had been doing his homework when the phone rang. The police had simply called the number on the back of the photo. His father had made some excuse about going to the office. But Tom knew really. He knew from the look on his father's face, from the tone of his voice, the way his father avoided eye contact, and the way he squeezed Tom's shoulder before he left. And he knew because he'd known for years, the way children do, even if they never form the sentences that contain the details of the truth, they feel it. And for all that his mother had disappointed him and finally abandoned him, they had shared a visceral connection. But at thirteen Tom was already adept at compartmentalizing, and so he went back to his homework.

It was closer to two hours before his dad returned. Tom had heard the key in the front door and waited. He'd turned the radio on for company, Joe Cocker crooning, "You are so beautiful to me." The tick of the clock on the mantle grew louder along with the beat of Tom's heart, the blood pounding in his ears. It was September, Indian summer, the dining room window open, the air sweetened by the rose briar his mother had planted the day Tom started kindergarten. It seemed to take forever for his father to come in to the room and when he did Tom didn't look up, but kept his head down in the history book, going over and over the same facts about the War of the Roses, as if to keep reading would ensure he would never have to hear what he knew his father was going to tell him.

Tom had sat dry-eyed, his arm around his father's shoulder, his eyes on the clock as it continued its forward measure of time.

Now he watched Kenneth, quietly weeping. The cotton handkerchief that Tom kept in his back pocket, and which he never used, had been his mother's. The police had found it in her hand. It had been a Mother's Day present from Tom when he was ten. His father gave it to him that night, and the next day, without washing it, Tom had ironed it; folding it in half and half again, the edges perfectly aligned, the iron sealing in the last of his mother's tears. He'd carried it in his back pocket for seventeen years now, and had still not used it, the tears for his mother, for himself, unspent. He reached for it now and held it out for Kenneth.

Charles looked on, the latest round of Ibuprofen and ice doing their job. He'd learned from Jocelyn the importance of not leaping in to make it all better. Had been admonished by her countless times before it finally sunk in that sometimes the best thing to do was just shut up and let the other person feel what they needed to feel. Obviously this had been a long time coming for Kenneth and although it made him feel uncomfortable, he felt something almost holy in the silence they kept. When Tom had given Kenneth his handkerchief, Charles had been close to tears himself.

How amazing, he thought, three grown men, dressed in bedspreads, mostly strangers to each other before this night had found, in the eye of this storm, a refuge with each other, a safety he would never have thought possible between men. Even as he was having these tender feelings he understood what Kenneth meant when he had said he was afraid that this night would end and everything he'd learned would end with it. Just like those mind-altering acid highs had evaporated back in the '60s. Would these revelations and kindnesses fade? And what had Charles learned? That he'd never come to terms with his father's death? That he'd given up the career he'd felt passionate about to please a woman incapable of loving him? That now he loved a woman whose capacity for love frightened him because he knew that one way or another it would end? If nothing else, death would claim it.

Once again the door to the lounge opened and Sarah stood hesitantly in the doorway dressed in men's overalls. Jocelyn gave her a gentle push and she took one step forward and stopped.

"Go on," Karenza said. "It won't hurt."

Tom turned to look at them, commenting on Sarah's attire. "This is turning into quite the transgender party," he said.

As Kenneth gave his nose a good blow and wiped his eyes, Sarah made her way to him and stood in front of him, unable to look at him. "I'm sorry," she said.

Kenneth looked up at her, and saw the name embroidered in red over her left breast. "How very civil of you, Harry," he said, attempting a joke.

Neither she nor Kenneth made eye contact. Sarah looked at her feet, her sensible pumps not seeming quite so sensible now that they were paired with overalls. Kenneth had gone back to staring at the fire, unable or unwilling to offer Sarah anything more. He was clearly uncomfortable just sitting there not acting, but there was something so determined about his silence, as though he had finally understood that no good would come of the customary civil response he'd always employed in an effort to diminish the consequences of the latest drunken hostilities. Yet as he held his nerve, it felt as though silence was the most powerful action he could take. Perhaps he would step off the old beaten track of habit? Sarah's body language said it all. "Please help me," it said, as if that's what she'd been trying to say all her life. But it was hard to tell whether she felt humble or humiliated and whether if she felt the latter she would want to lash out at Kenneth again and blame him for everything the way she had apparently never considered blaming her parents. Jocelyn came forward and led Sarah back to her chair and sat on the arm of it holding her hand. The room looked so cheery; the crackle of the fire, the warm glow of candlelight, even the chintz; although rain still beat against the window with its mournful plea to be let in.

"So," Karenza said. "Did we miss anything?"

"You mean the latest episode in the soap opera?" Tom muttered sarcastically.

"Actually, Karenza, I'd say 'kindness brought on by truth,' is the way I'd describe what has happened," Charles said, emotion still detectable in his voice.

"Oh, right," Karenza nodded. "So is civility a lost cause now?"

"No," Kenneth replied, still looking at the fire. "It's not a lost cause, just an excuse for avoiding the truth sometimes. To be honest, I still think it preferable to treat people with respect, but the problems arise when being civil becomes a pretense. Pretense is a lie; it doesn't change reality, it distorts it. I see that now."

"That's great for you. But what about us? What about where *we* are now?" Sarah pleaded, more engaged than anyone had expected.

Kenneth, seeming not to realize that Sarah was talking about them, continued with his global rant. "Do we really think the millennium will change everything? That we're all going to have some kind of global awakening and as the clock strikes midnight all the ills in the world will disappear? We'll have spent billions on spectacular celebrations and for a moment civilization will look really shiny. But that's not the truth. When the last stroke of midnight strikes it will really just be the dawn of another day. When it comes right down to it, the only thing I can believe in is me; I'd like to find out who that is before entropy carries me off."

There was a moment's awkward silence before Tom interrupted it.

"Do we have any votes for the validity of truth?" he asked, and everyone raised a hand.

29

The wind had picked up again, so much so that it was impossible, from within the lounge, to hear the grandfather clock strike its single note, although Tom jumped out of his skin when he returned from the kitchen with more wood and came abreast of the damn thing when it struck. He went up to it to see if it had chimed the half-hour or one o'clock in the morning and staring it in the face saw the elegant hands were semaphoring the latter.

That would make it eight in the evening in New York. Almost forty-eight hours since Tom had proposed to Lily. The proposal, if not the rejection, had already taken on a dreamlike quality. When he thought about it now he felt embarrassed and annoyed; the former for having made a fool of himself in public and the latter for having misread the inequality of their feelings for each other. But really, he wondered, was that true? Had he really loved Lily more than she had loved him? Indeed had he really loved her, or any other woman for that matter? Besides his mother, of course. Even she hadn't returned it in abundance. What the hell was love anyway? And how did one find it? He thought about the two couples on the other side of the door and, always one to run the percentages, saw the odds at two to one. With one arm loaded with logs, and the other carrying the torch, he kicked the door a couple of times with his foot and Karenza let him in.

"Ah," she said, "the return of the lumberjack."

Tom put the wood down next to the hearth, stoked the fire

and fed it two more logs. The room was quite warm and cosy now, if a little chillier than before the power failure, but compared with the rest of the inn, which was positively frigid, it was really quite pleasant.

"Do you think we need to worry about pipes freezing?" he asked.

"No, I don't think so," Karenza said. "It's cold but not cold enough for a freeze. That doesn't usually happen until January."

"It must be really bleak here then," Tom said.

"Hard to imagine anything bleaker than tonight," Charles said.

"Yeah, but we've got our love to keep us warm, right?" was Karenza's quick reply, and for a moment Tom couldn't tell if she was being flippant or if she meant it. Did she know what love was, he wondered? Somehow he doubted it. She didn't seem like someone who would let anyone that close. Perhaps they were kindred spirits after all. Sad that that the two youngest people in the room were the most jaded.

Jocelyn had made another pot of tea and was slicing pears and cheese. If it weren't for the strange attire of four of the six of them it would have looked a bit like a church social. "Are we expecting Father Christmas?" Tom asked, nodding towards three pairs of trousers that Jocelyn had hung at the mantelpiece, securing them with a stack of books

"Oh yes, I see what you mean! I just thought if we could dry them then the mud would brush off," Jocelyn said.

"Ah, the old brush off," Tom said and helped himself to some fruit before sitting back down. "How's the hand?" he asked Charles.

"Holding steady, as long as I don't move it too much."

Jocelyn had pulled a footstool over to the couch and was perched next to Charles holding his good hand to her cheek. She looked at Sarah quietly sitting in her chair, sipping tea. She looked shattered and pale and was probably desperate for a drink.

"Is anyone tired? D'you think we could manage to get a mattress down the stairs? It will just be too cold in the bedrooms."

"Tom and I could do that," Kenneth offered. "If there's a need. Anyone?" The murmured response from around the room was that everyone was OK for now. And so the merry little band settled in once more.

"So," Karenza said. "We've done God, impermanence slash entropy and civility slash truth. Three down, three to go."

"Are we sure we want to continue?" Jocelyn asked.

"Absolutely," Karenza said. "It'll be a breeze now."

"What makes you so sure?" Charles asked.

"Well how much worse could it get?" Karenza asked. "I would have thought we've used up the quota for *Sturm und Drang*. Maybe we can even things out a bit now." Karenza appeared to be looking forward to her turn, quietly confident perhaps that after what had gone before she would be good at arguing her case. "It's all right with me," Tom said; he had been on a fairly even keel all evening, and seemed quite unfazed. However, the faintest hesitation in Jocelyn did not go undetected. "How about you, Jocelyn? You're game aren't you?" She sighed then took in a deep breath, as though rousing herself from a reverie.

"OK," she said. "In for a penny in for a pound. Kenneth you pick."

Kenneth took the vase and reached inside. "Interesting," he said as read the piece of paper. "Ladies and gentlemen, I give you Equality."

> PART IV <

30

"Huh, if only you could," Karenza said, addressing Kenneth.

"Could what?" he asked.

"Give us equality," she replied.

"Why am I not surprised? I had you pegged for women's rights," Tom said.

"Well, obviously I'm for that, but actually it's children's rights I'm more interested in. It's my specialty in the degree I'm taking."

"So what are you doing? Some kind of social care thing?"

"Family law, actually."

"Ah, so it's not all about sexual discrimination for you, then?"

"You're a child before you're a woman and children are the single largest demographic when it comes to rights and equality. Children are the true victims."

"What do you mean by 'true victims'? Sounds a bit over-dramatic," Kenneth asked.

"It certainly isn't overdramatic. Children don't even have the most basic choices—like who they live with."

"How true," said Sarah quietly, as though she had only thought it and not said it out loud. How many nights for how many years had she lain in bed, as a child, trying to plot a way to leave home? She was five when she made her first and only attempt.

There were nineteen years between Sarah and Nancy her next sibling up. What happened after all those years that would have prompted an intimacy between Sarah's parents that had resulted in Sarah, the menopause baby, was anyone's guess.

It had been Nancy that little Sarah had decided she would run away to. Now, as Sarah sat sipping her tea, she wondered what had happened to that little girl who, in spite of having been thwarted, had shown more courage and resourcefulness than the adult Sarah could ever imagine having once possessed. She had saved the envelope that had housed Nancy's fifth birthday card to her, the address neatly printed on the back flap. And she had half a crown left over from Christmas. Thus armed, as she thought, with sufficient funds and a place to go, she had packed some clothes, a bag of Maltesers and her favourite Rupert book, and when evening crept through the curtains of her bedroom she had tiptoed down the stairs and out the back door.

She remembered the feelings of fearlessness and of freedom she'd experienced as she walked down the avenue, her little hand trailing the stone walls, still warm from the summer's day. Her parents had watched her from the front window. They had waited until she neared the end of the street and then her father had brought her home, his hand a lifeless weight around her little shoulders. He and her mother laughing at her before sending her back to her bedroom where her father put her over his knee, pulled down her knickers and smacked her bottom six times. No wonder then that for Sarah humiliation became forevermore the inescapable punishment attached to freedom.

"So, come on then, Karenza. You're the law student, make your case. What's your definition of equality?" Tom sat back in his chair and folded his arms, waiting to be persuaded or otherwise.

"Oh piss off. I haven't swallowed a dictionary you know!"

"OK, but you've got to lay out your stall, Karenza." Tom seemed to be looking forward to a little combat.

"Alright then. OK. I'd say equality is about being equal in status, rights and opportunity. Good enough for you?"

"Hear, hear! Well said," cried Jocelyn.

"Sounds like a reasonable definition," Tom responded. "But

you know, this strikes me as another one of those ideals. It's like Kenneth's idea about 'civilty'; it's nice in theory but it's idealistic to think it will ever be a reality for everyone."

"You know what," Karenza retorted. "You're one of those people who poo-poos idealism, but what's wrong with campaigning for things to be fairer, for a level playing field? The irony is you're a perfectionist. It's like nothing exists for you unless it's one hundred percent guaranteed."

"I'm with Karenza," Jocelyn said. "Surely some things are worth fighting for and equality must be the most fundamental right of all. It's like in the American Constitution. How does it go, Charles? Something about an unalienable right?"

Charles raised himself up a little on the couch and putting his good hand over his heart, quoted, "*We hold these truths to be self-evident, that all men are created equal and that they are endowed by their Creator, with certain unalienable rights, that among these are life, liberty and the pursuit of happiness.*"

"Nice," Karenza said. "But there are two things wrong with it."

"Really?" Charles said, "Enlighten me."

"Well, first of all it implies that only those who believe in a creator, and let's not be coy, your forefathers were referring to God, to *their* God … the old bearded protestant fucker. So, only those who believe in him get to be 'endowed' with the unalienable right to equality. Now *there's* an amendment to your Constitution begging to be enacted. So, my learned friend," Karenza addressed Charles with a wry twist of her mouth. "perhaps the court could ask for your repetition of the text omitting the phrase '*by their creator.*' It would be a great step towards equality."

"Point taken," Charles said.

"What's the second thing?" Tom said.

"Men," Sarah interjected. "It says only men are created equal."

The entire group turned to her, surprised that she was still conscious, but even more so that she had grasped so fine a point.

"Bingo, Sarah," Karenza said. "Exactly right. So, according to the American Constitution, only men who believe in God have the right to equality!"

"But it's not just a gender thing," Charles reflected. "For whatever reason, non-Aryans were not equals during the Holocaust. But then nor were homosexuals, Aryan or otherwise. However you look at it," he continued, "if enough people anywhere share a common fear they are easily roused to treat 'others' as unequal; whether it's men and women, Christians and Jews, blacks and whites, straight versus gay. What gets me is that the biggest majority of all—the poor—let the rich minority have all the power."

"I think we'd all like to understand that one, darling," Jocelyn kissed his hand.

"So as a Jew, do *you* feel equal?" Karenza continued to favour the direct approach.

"God. Now you've taken me right back to seventh grade!" Charles winced at the memory. "Upper East Side. John Phillips. What a shit he was. I'd been one of the boys until I knocked him out of first place in class." Charles remembered every detail of the afterschool attack. They'd called him "Moses, kike, dirty Jew." Overnight he'd become the common enemy. "The worst thing was my best buddy not sticking up for me. He ran off the first sign of trouble. That hurt." But had he felt unequal?

"D'you know what? I don't base my identity on being Jewish," he said. "It is only one of many aspects of who I am. If I only identified with my Jewishness I would probably either be arrogant or feel unequal. If you had asked if I ever experienced prejudice, I would have said yes." There was a moment of silence as the grandfather clock struck two, the chimes somehow redolent of history and its inevitable claim on the present.

"I was deeply saddened that day," Charles continued. "And frightened. But I can't say I felt unequal to anyone. Frankly, I may even have felt a tad superior. But my father was appalled. This was New York, the New World, this sort of thing wasn't supposed to happen here, and certainly not to his son. For him it wasn't enough that the headmaster made the boys apologize; he wanted revenge. And for him that meant I had to be better than them. It was a lonely year, let me tell you." He paused for a moment. The ice bag was now water and he removed it and sat up a little on the couch. He turned to Karenza, "Do you think there's any more ice left in the kitchen?" he asked.

"I'll go and look," Tom offered, apparently glad to have a reason to get away. Perhaps one didn't have to be judged by others in order to feel unequal?

Angling the torch into the freezer, Tom used his other hand to fill one of the small white bin-liners with a bunch of cubes and suddenly felt disoriented. Was it just a couple of hours ago that he'd been wearing these bags on his feet? Everything that had happened since dinner seemed to expand and collapse, as though time was an oceanic pulse that rose and fell according to its own unmetered rhythm, a rhythm that would never equal the reasoned measure of the clock.

What was it about feeling equal? He'd felt unequal most of his life. His mother was a drunk and then she died. That set him apart and he still felt it now. Why else was he so aloof and judgmental? Because he felt judged himself? Yet Charles had suffered prejudice but refused to experience himself as unequal. This was alien to Tom, and even as he was thinking it, he experienced himself as inferior. When he got back to the lounge he gave the bag of ice to Jocelyn, even though he had the desire to minister to Charles personally, as if to do so would bring him closer to being like him.

"Hey Tom, you missed something!" Karenza said, turning to him, "Kenneth, tell Tom."

"Well, we were just talking about comparison," Kenneth said, "and how we tend to judge others? I mean, comparison is the basis of inequality isn't it? You know that thing about *'all animals are equal but some are more equal than others*'? So I thought we could each of us give an example of how we judge others to be less equal."

Kenneth had clearly been bitten by the truth bug, but the discomfort in the room was palpable. "How much nicer it is to just stick with examples of how one has been judged and been done wrong by, rather than putting the searchlight on one's own prejudices."

"Well, I'm guilty as hell," Charles said. "I'm a doctor, so I'm God." The others laughed, glad of a little light relief. "No, but seriously," Charles went on, "and really I don't like to admit this, but I don't treat my patients as equals. I really do believe I know better than them."

"Well, but you do," Jocelyn said, coming to his defense. She had an investment in seeing him as one of the few caring physicians she'd ever met.

"Well, medically, scientifically, maybe. But who am I to say I know what's best for someone else? And you know what? I often decide what to tell or not tell a patient in order to get them to follow the treatment I deem best for them. If I were really to treat them as equals I would have to give them all the facts and then ask them what they thought, how they felt, what they would like to do. But you know, when patients don't do what I want them to do I judge them to be inferior."

Kenneth put another couple of logs on the fire. One of the candles on the mantelpiece, perhaps due to the heat of the fire, had burned down and Karenza lit another and stuck it in the melted wax. There were two bottles of water left and she asked if anyone would like more tea. Charles opted for plain water, but the rest of them were eager for the comfort of another pot and some more biscuits and chocolate.

Jocelyn dunked her digestive in the tea and as she ate the softened biscuit, mused for a moment. "Gosh," she said. "This is an interesting exercise. We all make hundreds of judgments every day that we don't even think about, right?" She dunked her biscuit again. "You know, the sort of thing" she said. "My guilty thing is that—because I'm English, naturally—I always think the English way is best. Only in England could something as plain and whole-some as this biscuit be valued. In America it would have to be cream-filled and slathered in chocolate because (I judge) Ameri-cans are lacking in taste. I do that all the time. It's like what I am as an English person only has value if I belittle Americans. It's the same thing when we make random judgments about people we don't even know. How many times a day do we put people down by silently judging their clothes or their haircut? Every time we do that we're basically saying we're better than them."

"Aren't we getting a little off track here?" Tom said, well aware that he was supremely guilty of the type of prejudice Jocelyn was talking about. "I would imagine," he said, "that Karenza had something bigger in mind when she chose equality."

"But doesn't prejudice start with the little things?" Jocelyn asked. "Surely if we can judge a stranger for their haircut or a patient for not agreeing to a doctor's advice, then how big a step is it to judging someone for their race or religion or gender?"

Staring into their mugs of tea, everyone in the room went a little quiet for a moment.

"What do you think, Karenza?" Charles asked.

"Well, I agree with Jocelyn, actually, but we are getting away from what I was driving at."

"Which is what?" Charles asked.

"Well, OK. What about a deeply ingrained, unequal view of the world that allows people to mistreat others?"

"You mean like slavery for example?" Charles asked.

"Absolutely," Karenza said. "I mean, what exactly was it about black skin that frightened us whities so much that the only way we could deal with our fear was to denigrate blacks and then make them do our dirty work? And let's face it," she continued, "blacks still aren't equal are they, any more than women are?"

"Oh, but we've made tremendous progress, don't you think?" Kenneth chipped in. "Blacks and women can vote now, they can go to any school they want, they can apply for the same jobs ..."

"Yes," Karenza interrupted. "But the women won't get equal pay. It's easy for people to get all smug about progress, but it's not enough."

"She's right, Kenneth," Charles said. "I doubt that the African American who graduated top of his class at Harvard feels like enough progress toward equality has been made when a taxi driver refuses to pick him up, or a white woman crosses the street at night when she sees him coming toward her."

The room went silent. It was as if depression had seeped in under the sill. As though the oppression of inequality from the small examples in their own lives to the enormity of it on a global scale was set before them. How could it be that civilization had come far enough to have invented the Internet and its supposed democratic liberation for all and yet still we insisted on treating each other so cruelly? For every step of progress towards equality, it seemed there was an even bigger step backward.

"Just yesterday," Kenneth added, "I read an article about how the Internet was being used to peddle young girls into prostitution, never mind that anyone can now get instructions via the web on how to make bombs, for chrissakes. It makes you want to build a cabin in the woods!"

"What about me?" Sarah ejaculated, clearly surprised that she was still conscious at two thirty in the morning. She was in need of a drink, but this inequality thing had been hammered into her all her life. From being the unwanted child, to the outcast in school because she was the goody-goody vicar's daughter, or to being the only kid who had parents old enough to be her grandparents. Then of course there had been falling in love with a man who was on the rebound, and being unable to bear children. Even as a military wife she hadn't felt equal; the other wives were either more vivacious, or ambitious or adventurous, or their husbands were of a higher rank, or they got posted to exotic places. And now, Sarah sat in front of everyone dressed in handyman's overalls, facing the backs of the rest of the group. Was this to be her position for the rest of her life, to be always sitting on the outside filling up with resentment until it suffocated her? She wanted, oh, how she wanted, to pick up her chair and move it into the semicircle. But what she wanted even more was for one of them to do it for her. Just for once to have someone invite her in, to say here, come here, you're one of us.

She looked towards the window where the rain still streamed, the world an unreachable blur, and an urge arose in her to run at the window, to fly through it, the glass shards parting for her like velvet curtains opening onto the final act. She felt herself get up, felt her heart beating through the walls of her chest in an attempt at escape just as she'd felt when she was five years old. The air squeezing out of her lungs, she heard the sound of her voice as she flew out, over the cliff, over the sea, the sky cracking with lightning and then, the soft dark embrace.

31

....

"Sarah, Sarah, can you hear me . . . ?" Kenneth was on his knees, patting her cheek. "My God," he said, "I think she's had a heart attack."

The rest of the group had gotten up and were standing in a circle around her. Charles, in spite of his hand, was down on his knees on the other side of Sarah, checking her pulse rate, raising an eyelid, monitoring her colour. "It's not a heart attack," he said. "More like a severe panic attack. Has she had them before?" he asked Kenneth.

"Not as far as I know."

"We need to get her comfortable in front of the fire," he said. "Maybe now's the time to bring down a mattress?" Tom and Karenza immediately offered to sort this out.

Jocelyn put a cushion under Sarah's head and held one hand while Kenneth held the other.

"Charles, darling, you should look after your hand and go back to the couch," Jocelyn said. "You can give us instructions from there."

Sarah opened her eyes and saw her husband and sister-in-law looking at her with concern. The absence of judgment made her weep. It was as though she were a child again, but with two caring parents looking at her.

"What happened?" she asked.

"Charles says you had a panic attack," Kenneth said, and then making light of it, added, "and we all know the doctor's always right."

"I thought I was having a heart attack," she said. "I thought I was dying. It was so lonely."

"It's all right, Sarah," Jocelyn said, stroking her brow. "You're all right. We're all here."

"Give her some water," Charles said, "but sit up slowly, Sarah."

Jocelyn got the water and Kenneth helped her sit up. She was heavy and weak and there was nothing to prop her up with so he sat behind her and putting his legs on either side of her, holding her against his chest. He felt her soften against him, felt surrender, his own as much as hers. The last time he'd held a woman like this was before Sarah.

It had been a late summer day. He was twenty-five and in love with Suzanna Mason. He could see her now. Wild Suzanna, with her dark curls and reckless eyes. Suzanna, who teased him and brought out the adventurer in him. He'd just bought a second-hand Morris Minor and they had taken it on its maiden voyage to Sandbanks. He was on leave, she'd played truant from work. They had the beach to themselves. She dared him to go in the water, but he demurred, telling her he didn't have a swimsuit with him. Who needs a swimsuit, she'd said and he'd watched as she stood up and stripped, the sun behind her outlining her silhouette in gold, her pubic hair a wild nest of black curls, and then she'd turned from him and ran to the sea, shrieking with joy as the first wave hit her. He'd followed her, as he thought he would follow her all his life, his nakedness a freedom, as if he finally inhabited his own skin. He ran towards her, his erection preceding him. He was invincible. He entered the sea and then he entered her and for the first time, the image of his father didn't appear. She was the siren and the sea swelled around them, each wave vying for their submission and they rose and fell and the seagulls wheeled overhead urging them on and finally the future was his, unimpeded by the past.

He'd toweled her down with his undershirt and helped her get dressed, himself still naked, his penis shriveled from the sea, yet even so coming back to life as he dressed himself. The sun went behind a cloud. Her teeth chattered. He led her to a sand dune, leaned back against it and, spreading his legs on either side of her had cradled her against his chest.

"I'm pregnant," she said, and for a stupid moment he thought they had just conceived a child; a water baby born of passion and the sea. But then the stupid moment spun away as the realization that they had never made love before brought with it the terrible truth. He sat there, stunned. The woman he was holding in his arms deflated and was gone. He pushed her away and ran, ran down the beach, along the edge of the sea where he had so recently spent himself, the pain of all that he had just had and lost, inescapable, unbearable. And when he got back to the dune it was hollow and she was gone and he lay there and wept until the sun went down.

Now, as he held Sarah, he felt shame. Shame that he had chosen a woman whom he could judge as inferior to him in order that he could be in control. He remembered Jocelyn once talking about how making amends was an important part of becoming sober and as he sat there cradling Sarah and feeling, for the first time, her vulnerability, he realized he had some amends to make himself.

32

....

Karenza and Tom closed the door behind them and made their way to the stairs.

"See what you escaped?" Karenza said. "There's thirty years of marriage for you."

Even in the dark he was aware of her body, and as they climbed the stairs he wanted to reach for her. If she had been wearing a skirt he thought, he could have reached up underneath it. Instead he sensed the movement of her hips and then surprisingly caught a waft of his cologne.

"I gather you're not into marriage," he said.

"No, thanks." They had reached the landing and she turned to him, "I've never seen one I like and those two are no exception."

"What about Charles and Jocelyn?"

"They're not married, are they?"

"What about children?" he asked.

"What about them?"

"Do you want to have any?"

"Absolutely not."

"What do you want?"

"The same as you," she said. "A successful career, but unlike you money is not important to me. Making a difference is what I'm interested in."

"What makes you think money is important to me?" he asked, defensively.

"Everything about you. Your clothes, your shoes, your Hermès address book. You even read about money in bed."

"Is there anything in my room you didn't check out?"

"Not really," she said. "Too bad you weren't in it. I could have checked you out, too." She laughed.

"Now's your chance," he said and taking what he thought to be a cue, he reached out and pulled her to him. The bedspread, which he was wearing like a sarong, came loose and fell to the floor and he suddenly felt incredibly vulnerable as though they had switched roles and he was the woman. And once again Karenza dominated, as she grabbed his arse with both hands. He reached for her mouth, but she turned her face away.

"For someone who believes in equality you sure like to have the upper hand," he said and removing hers, retrieved the bedspread and retied it around his waist. "Let's get the mattress."

"Men don't generally like it when women have the upper hand," Karenza said, turning from him and making her way to the room with the twin beds.

Tom had been standing close to her, and he could sense Karenza's tension. What was it about her? She was so bold in some ways, but when it came to down to it, she was reserved in the extreme. He recognized a cock-teaser when he saw one, but that wasn't her. She seemed to want to create situations and then shut them down. And he started to wonder what had been done to her. What safeguards had been breached that made her act this way? She was still too young, too unformed and yet full of the self-righteousness of youth to be this cynical. Had she ever experienced the one place where men and women could come together as equals, in the wordless act of making love, where desire had the opportunity to meet desire? This sacred meeting place, which for so many people was the place of missed opportunity, and may be for Karenza was a howling cave of violation. What Tom couldn't know was that the little girl who had been chosen to be a snowflake in her ballet school's production of *The Nutcracker* had been dirtied; her joyous physicality translated by misuse into provocation, her ability to provoke worn now like a cloak beneath which she held the dagger of revenge.

But Tom was feeling his own needs. He'd like to show her a thing or two about equality. Who did she think she was, that she could flaunt and retract her sexuality at will? She was the type they were talking about when they said a girl was asking for it. Not that he believed anyone deserved to be raped. He followed her into the bedroom where she was already stripping one of the twin beds.

"Let's take the mattress down first," she said. "Then I'll come back for the sheets and blankets."

As he reached for the mattress he wondered if it bore the stains of requited love. He thought of Lily, of his mother, and then, feeling Karenza's unreachable presence in the darkness, wondered what it was about him that invited rejection.

"I'll take this," he said, pulling the mattress off the frame. "Wouldn't want you getting too close to the residue of other people's sex," he said and dragged its unyielding body out of the room.

Back in the lounge, the room had achieved the ambience of a turn of the last century drawing room and coming back to it, even after just a few minutes away collecting more logs, Kenneth felt comfortable. He recognized the tolerance that had grown between them. Maybe it had to do with their dependency on each other. With the exception of his wife, he felt that whatever difficulties they might all have, they could all be counted on to help each other through the night. And he felt, at this point, that the worst had been done, that the darts and cruelties that had been aimed at each other were spent; now they were out of ammunition and most of them had revealed their secrets and defects, there was nothing left to be afraid of. He thought that what had started out as a ridiculous game now had the possibility of becoming a mature discussion that might even bring a measure of enlightenment along with the dawn. And once again, as soon as he thought about the night ending, he felt sadness and fear. Once the bridge was fixed and they were free to leave, he'd be on his own again with an alcoholic wife. He knew from years in the military that crisis brought one's fellow soldiers together. It had nothing to do with camaraderie; it was the basic instinct that only by coming together and working in harmony could the crisis be survived. Yet the feeling of kinship that he had felt in those times had always been shattered once the crisis ended. He knew how quickly one forgot, how easily one returned to familiar patterns of judgment and distance. Is that what the dawn would bring? Would his newly vulnerable wife retreat into her addiction? Would the closeness and respect he felt for Charles disappear at daybreak? And what about his sister, the person he now realized he'd always seen as ruining his existence? Torn between protection and resentment, he'd masked his agony by coming to judge her; for her relationships, her parenting, her alcoholism. Then when she'd become sober and found Charles, he'd been left with resentment. The resentment building until tonight, when he'd viewed her as a self-serving relative who managed to spare him a couple of days once a year. What would happen to them when morning came a-knocking? He watched as Tom and Karenza moved the semicircle of furniture a little bit back from the fire to make room for his wife. Watched as Karenza, with a tenderness he'd not thought possible, made the bed with Jocelyn, as if the two of them were playing dolls. And then he and Tom helped Sarah up and walked her slowly to the bed, lowering her like a baby. Jocelyn put an extra pillow under her head and Karenza put a cup of tea next to her on the hearth, and then everyone resumed their places and watched as Sarah turned from them to watch the flames, caught somewhere between shame and joy.

The wind and rain were by now a combined force that

had taken on an almost biblical dimension in that it seemed wrought by an invisible power whose wrath could obliterate them at will.

"So does anyone have any thoughts on why we have beliefs in the first place?" Jocelyn asked. "I mean why do we need to believe in something? For instance, what made you choose equality as the *one* thing you believe in Karenza? Was it something your family believed in? Where did that come from?"

Karenza began to laugh, controlled it and then began again. She tried to answer but every time she began to speak she laughed harder until it wasn't funny anymore. Everyone was looking at her; even Sarah had turned from the fire, the sound of Karenza's laughter connecting with her own anxiety. She wanted Karenza to stop. If she had the energy she would have gotten up and slapped her face. Couldn't everyone else see the girl was hysterical?

"What's so funny?" Tom asked, feeling slightly unnerved. This young woman who'd been so brazen all evening, who'd pushed so many buttons while remaining in control of her own emotions, suddenly seemed on the very edge of cracking. What was going on? Was she bipolar, or what? It seemed so out of character.

Tears were running down Karenza's cheeks when she finally stopped laughing. She went over to the drinks trolley and grabbed a couple of napkins, wiping her eyes as she sat back down.

"If you must know, the only example of equality in my family," she said, "were my identical twin brothers."

"OK. Older or younger?" asked Charles.

"Chronologically they're five years older," she said, "but emotionally they're more like three-year-olds."

"Do they live here in Cornwall?" Jocelyn asked.

"No, they're in London, supposedly running a night club. I don't even want to think about what else they may be running." She had regained her composure to the point where she seemed totally devoid of any emotion, as though she was talking about someone else's family.

Sarah, who had earlier enjoyed her role as the drunken shit-stirrer, sensed something in Karenza that she didn't want to know about. She fervently wished everyone would stop asking her questions, but Tom, also sensing something and wanting to get even, pushed ahead.

"And what do your parents do?" he asked.

"Not that it's relevant, but my mother is an estate agent. My father is in jail."

"Oh," Tom said. "So like a guard or a warden or something?"

"An inmate," Karenza said, looking him straight in the eye as if daring him to equal that.

Once again the room plummeted into silence. The wind and rain were deafening and the crackle of the fire electric in intensity, while the fourth element seemed to have been snatched away. Whatever ground had felt firm beneath their feet was now a fault-line with five people teetering on one side while the sixth stood immovable on the other, between them a chasm opened its hungry mouth.

"What's the matter?" Karenza said looking at each of them in turn. "Doesn't anyone want to know why he's in jail?"

"Yes," Jocelyn said. "I do."

"He's a rapist."

Sarah gasped and Karenza turned on her, "Oh, poor little Sarah, you think you've had it so bad don't you? You thought you had the edge on suffering, eh? You thought there was nothing worse than losing babies, right? All of you, you make me sick with your little stories of pain. Poor Charles, the Jew-boy. Poor Jocelyn, the bastard child. Oh poor Kenneth and Jocelyn with your naughty daddy who fucked the sister. And Sarah, with her daddy, the wicked vicar who diddles the boys. You want to switch, Sarah? You want my daddy instead? How would you like that, eh? You want a daddy who fucks young girls? Better still, how about a daddy who fucks you first? Think you could handle that,

Sarah?" she said, leaning over her, her face redder than her hair, the veins on her neck blue streaks on alabaster, threads of spittle flying from her mouth, her body quivering. She stood there, the personification of years of rage let loose, "Everyone equal now?" she screamed and fled the room.

33

The door slammed. The wind stopped. Jocelyn reached for Charles's hand while Kenneth and Tom looked at each other, swiftly turning away as if they couldn't bear to see another representative of the male species. Tom flushed deep red remembering how he had, so recently, thought girls like Karenza deserved what they got.

"How awful," Kenneth said, in recognition of what Karenza had suffered, but also as a reprimand to himself for having thought about how Karenza reminded him of his aunt.

"There's something to be said for impermanence after all," Charles said, quietly squeezing Jocelyn's hand since she was evidently in shock.

"Well that proves there's no God," Sarah commented bluntly.

The clock struck three and as the last chime vibrated into the night, Jocelyn stood up and made for the door.

"Where are you going?" Charles asked.

"Where do you think?" she said. "The girl's broken."

"I'll come with you," Kenneth said, getting to his feet.

"No," Jocelyn shouted. "I'm sorry, but I don't think a man is what she needs right now."

When she opened the lounge door a blast of cold air came at her. At first she thought it was just the chill of the unheated house, but then she realized it was wind that she was feeling and turning towards it saw that the front door to the inn was wide open.

For a moment she told herself there was nothing to worry about, that Karenza had just gone out to cool down, to gain control of herself again and that it would be better to just go back to the lounge and wait for her. It wasn't that she was afraid of the dark, or even of the storm; she was afraid of what she might find. Yet at the same time she felt impelled to go. Felt that perhaps this was the one opportunity she might have to be there for a young woman in a way she had never been there for her daughter.

As she closed the front door behind her, she prayed that it hadn't locked and berated herself for not having taken a torch. Although the wind had abated somewhat, the rain drenched her to the skin within seconds. She began calling Karenza's name the way a mother calls for a disappeared child. She had some memory of the grounds of the inn from her stay there with Charles the previous year, although then they had been lush with the foliage and blossoms of June. She knew there was a small arbor on the lounge side of the house and thought maybe Karenza had gone there for some semblance of shelter, but as she rounded the corner of the house she saw the downed power line sparking and hissing on the wet ground.

She turned back towards the car park in the hope of finding her safe inside one of the cars, but there weren't any parked. There were only two other directions to go; towards the washed out bridge or the cliff edge. She started towards the bridge searching for a legitimate reason as to why Karenza might go there knowing all the while that she hadn't. She was crying as she turned back and headed towards the cliff; crying and calling out for Karenza. How could the night be so dark and yet the sky not be black? How could a person as bold as Karenza make such a frail mark in the landscape? How could Jocelyn reach her before she jumped? Why did she have to be the one to try and save her? And if she didn't, how would she herself survive? Would she survive or would Karenza take her with her? Was this to be her final test?

She was shivering as much from terror of what may be about to happen as from the cold rain. And then something let go in her. It was as if hope and expectation were vanquished and all that was left was animal instinct. She took off her boots and sprinted across the muddy grass like a jaguar, her eyes never leaving the back of Karenza's neck, which she now had in her sights. Hurling herself through the night, through time, through history, she was unaware of space, of the sea's fast approach. She was only aware of the line that was the cliff's edge. She knew it was a line that had been drawn for her, that it was one she didn't want to cross, would not cross. Her hand grabbed the neck of Karenza's shirt ripping it, and as Karenza tilted forward Jocelyn's other hand grabbed her hair and pulled her back on to her so that they fell to the ground, screaming. Karenza was like an upturned insect struggling to right herself.

"Let me go! Let me go!" She punched at Jocelyn with her elbows, one of them catching Jocelyn under the jaw so that her teeth went into her lip. Her left hand lost its grip on Karenza's hair who was now turning and flailing and scratching and screaming and howling. Jocelyn held her now as she continued to scream.

"No more, no more, let me go . . ." and as she beat Jocelyn's ribs, Jocelyn held on. She held on to all of the fury.

"Yes," she said. "It's OK, Karenza. Let me have it, yes," and she felt Karenza's body surrender, the deep shuddering sobs going right through both of them as she held her and rocked her in the lashing rain at the edge of the abyss.

34

It was Sarah who first expressed concern, not only for Karenza but also for Jocelyn. What if Karenza had decided to hurl herself over the cliff, and Jocelyn had gone after her? If she had suffered what Karenza had suffered herself, she'd probably have offed herself a long time ago. The girl was right; what were her pains and losses compared to being raped by your own father? It was bad enough that she and Kenneth had fathers who had disgraced themselves and their families but to have your body violated by the person who was supposed to protect you seemed to Sarah to leave no possibility of recovery. And where were the mothers? Her own, Kenneth's and Jocelyn's, Karenza's? What part had they played in these horrors? Where had they been when their children most needed them?

"It must have been at least ten minutes," she said. "I'm really worried. Don't you think we should look for them?"

"Look, I know what you're thinking, but Jocelyn's really good in this situation. She'll be talking to Karenza somewhere safe ... They just need a little time." Charles couldn't put into words what each of them secretly feared, that Karenza had jumped. "Look, if anything bad had happened, Jocelyn would have been back for help by now." What he refused to consider was the possibility that they were both lying at the bottom of the cliff.

Kenneth was busying himself with the fire stabbing at the logs with the poker. Why was it that whenever he thought the worst was over, it never was? It was the first time in all the years that he'd felt protective of his sister that the feeling wasn't accompanied by resentment.

"I'm sure they're both fine. But what if they've gone outside? They'll be drenched," Tom said.

"And freezing," Sarah added. "We need to gather up the towels and blankets."

"I'm going out there to look for them. This is ridiculous," Kenneth flung down the poker and made his way towards the lounge door. "There's a torch in the kitchen still."

It was agreed that Tom would check the hotel while Kenneth would scour the grounds and bring them to the kitchen door if he found them, but then Sarah insisted that she would take over from there. Whatever traces of alcohol, panic and victimhood were left in her system had apparently been eradicated by a clear sense of purpose. An opportunity had presented itself for her to put others before herself and she was entirely focused on what needed to be done for Karenza and Jocelyn. It was as though an inkling of awareness took root in her, that she needed to hang on to this moment, in case it proved to be fleeting.

"Are you sure you're up for this?" Kenneth asked.

"Yes," she said, and the searching look that passed between them was one that neither seemed familiar with. Not the swiftly averted glance or the scathing stares at each other's backs, but a simple look of question and answer, of concern and reassurance.

Kenneth guided Sarah through to the kitchen while Tom went to check for them inside and gather supplies.

"There's no sign of them in here. Are you sure you can manage?" Tom asked having returned with a pile of towels and blankets.

"Yes," she said, "I just hope I do it right."

He squeezed her arm, "I'm sure you will," he said. "I'm leaving everything here," he added, putting the pile down on the kitchen island. And as he turned and left, that sentence reverberated in her. She muttered it to herself over and over like a mantra as she peered through the rain slashed window of the door. She could make out a faint pool of light from Kenneth's torch. Sarah pressed her face closer to the window and saw what looked like one small figure coming through the darkness. A flutter of panic rose in her. Then she saw it was both of them; Jocelyn holding Karenza up, partially carrying her; Karenza clinging to her, both of them crying. Kenneth hung back simply lighting the way. Sarah opened the door and immediately wrapped a large towel around them, ushering Kenneth out of the room. Karenza slid out of Jocelyn's arms to the floor, her teeth juddering, her body shaking violently. "Please, oh, please, please help me." And the older women cooed like mourning doves. "Karenza, we're going to get these wet things off," Sarah said gently. Karenza cried harder. "It's all right, it's all right, it's just us, no one's going to hurt you now." While Jocelyn held on to Karenza, Sarah spread a blanket on the floor and put another towel on top of it. Then she unlaced the sodden boots and pulled them off. She carefully peeled off her tee shirt and undid the bra. But then as they unzipped the girl's jeans she screamed, a sound that no horror movie could ever hope to replicate. "It's all right, Karenza, it's me, Jocelyn, you're all right, it's all right," and the girl's body curled into the fetal position, her cries rending the women's hearts as they dried her with the towel before swaddling her in the blanket.

"Hold her while I get out of my clothes," Jocelyn said.

"Don't leave me," Karenza sobbed.

"It's okay, sweet girl, I'm right here," Sarah said, and sat on the floor cradling the girl in her arms. "Hush little baby," she crooned, "Hush little baby, don't you cry . . ."

35

Having seen the state of Karenza, Kenneth suggested to the others that it might be more appropriate if they vacated the lounge so that Karenza could get dry and warm in purely female company.

"You're absolutely right," Tom agreed and set about banking the fire with more logs, checking the candles. Finally, he filled the kettle with bottled water and put it back on the grate and smoothed the bedcovers on the mattress.

"Could one of you secure my skirt," Charles lisped, allowing his relief to show. His blanket had come untucked at the waist and with one hand out of commission, he was unable to fix it himself. Kenneth obliged, remarking that he thought it most unfair that an American had ended up with a tartan blanket while he and Tom were stuck with pink chenille and lilac candlewick.

"It's the McMorgan plaid," Charles said, making a butchered attempt at a Highland accent.

Kenneth moaned in mock agony.

"Oh, don't get upset Kenneth, you make such a lovely Widow Twanky," Tom joked.

"And I suppose you fancy yourself as Cinderella," Kenneth retorted. "The trousers are still damp but at least our socks are dry," he said, retrieving them from the mantelpiece. "We'll need these for the frozen tundra."

And off they padded in their finery, out into the chilly reception and down the hall to the bar. Tom opened the door and immediately stepped back as if hit by gale force winds.

"What the fuck . . ."

"Oh, my God," Charles said. "What the hell is that?"

There was an awkward pause.

"I'm afraid that's probably my wife," Kenneth said, trying not to gag.

"Whoa," Charles said, breathing through his mouth, "she really was far gone, eh?"

"Even for her," Kenneth said.

"OK," Tom said, shutting the door, "been there, done that. How about we go up to my room?"

"I thought you'd never ask," Charles said, combining lisp and brogue.

"Hang on," Kenneth said. "I'll get the torch and a couple of candles."

"Bring the scotch too," Charles said.

"And the chocolate," Tom added.

"Why don't I whip up a soufflé while I'm at it," Kenneth said, hitching up his skirt.

"Do you want a hand?" Charles asked.

"Well, since you've only got the one, no thanks."

"I'll come with you," Tom said,

"Just hurry up for fuck's sake," Charles said. "I'm freezing my Scottish balls off here."

Five minutes later the three men were sitting side by side in bed with the duvet pulled up to their chins, swigging scotch right out of the bottle. Although the wind had died down somewhat, the rain was insistent on the small paned window, dividing the sea and sky into nine frames of bleak abstraction. In the distance the lighthouse blinked its green signal, a tiny tease to "go" where none of them had ever been.

"If it clears up in the next couple of days it would be jolly nice to take a boat over there," Kenneth said, nodding his head in the direction of Godrevy.

"Send me a postcard," Tom said. "I'm getting the first train out of here."

"Not much of an adventurer, are you?" Kenneth said. "What about you, Charles?"

"Hospital first for me," he said.

"Oh, of course," Kenneth said, feeling a twinge of sadness.

They passed the bottle one more time before capping and putting it on the bedside table. As Kenneth put the bottle down he saw the faint white glow of open pages and asked Tom what he was reading.

"*The Return of Depression Economics*," he said.

"A bit of motivational reading before sleep, eh?" Charles said.

"It's my job to know how global economics are trending," Tom said, just a little defensively. "For my money, this guy Krugman is one of the most brilliant economists of our day. He's called a lot of things ahead of time."

"You don't say?"

"Frankly, if the US Government was smart they'd hire him as Treasurer, but the government's run by the banks, so there's no way they'd offer it to him. Anyway, he's too honourable for politics," he continued. "Any notion of equity is dead in the water."

"Why do you say that?" Charles asked.

"Because the whole system is gamed. You know that. Corporations and banks have been running the show for decades. It's the same everywhere. Politicians aren't in government to help people rise up; they don't care about education and health and equal rights. That doesn't work for them. They're too busy positioning themselves with the lobbyists so they can quit politics and become lobbyists themselves. If they spent their time trying to help people that would mean less of the pie for them."

"God, you really are a cynic, aren't you?" Kenneth said.

"No, I'm a realist."

And a lonely one at that, thought Charles, who wasn't in the mood for depression economics or depression anything. Believing in entropy did not, in his opinion, equal cynicism. If anything it made him want to enjoy the good times while they lasted. His hand was throbbing again and, again, he wondered if perhaps his days as a surgeon really were over. As the thought went through his mind he realized it didn't have the frisson of fear that it had just a couple of hours ago. Time, as ever, was moving forward and, as the saying goes, it and the tide wait for no man. Maybe he could let himself be carried in a different direction. Maybe he didn't even have to know what that direction was. Maybe he could persuade Jocelyn to take a sabbatical and the two of them could spend a year following their guts instead of institutional agendas.

Back in the kitchen, Jocelyn had toweled off and wrapped herself in a blanket. Sarah was still on the floor cradling Karenza, who by now had stopped crying. It was as though she were numb, not only from the cold and exhaustion, but from the lack of tension that had evidently been integral to her life for the last ten years. She seemed devoid of energy not even sufficient to rebuff the kindness she was being given. She lay in Sarah's arms, her head against Sarah's ample breast as though she might just fade away there, the perfect place to die. There, in the arms of a woman whom she had so recently judged as pitiful, maybe she finally understood that everyone's pain was equal.

36

....

After a while Jocelyn and Sarah convinced Karenza that they needed to get back to the lounge, but only after Jocelyn returned from a recce and could tell her that the menfolk had taken themselves off elsewhere. For Jocelyn, after the cold and the rain and the terror of outside, the lounge felt like a homecoming.

"They've made it nice. The fire's lovely and they've got the mattress right up close."

They helped Karenza onto her feet and gently made their way from the freezing cold kitchen back to their cosy cocoon. Sarah took charge, getting Karenza tucked in on the mattress, and putting the girl's sodden boots in front of the fire to dry. Jocelyn rubbed her arms up and down briskly to get the circulation going again and then made a hot toddy of tea and brandy for Karenza. As she poured it, Sarah looked sheepishly at Jocelyn, "I really want one, too," she said.

"I know," Jocelyn said. "Believe me, this is the first time in a long time that I've felt tempted myself. But you know what, it would do us both so much more harm than good. Make us a nice cup of tea and some cheese and biscuits."

Jocelyn's teeth were chattering, and she felt so cold it hurt. She knew she was in shock. She kept seeing Karenza's silhouette at the edge of the cliff, as though she were still there, as though she still had to save her. As she watched Sarah hold the toddy to Karenza's lips, she felt a deep resentment that what was an age-old remedy for some was for her pure poison. Even after all these years, she had only to see a bottle of brandy and she could taste it; that husky, amber, ballsy liquid that had been her courage for so long. But daily AA meetings had ruined the possibility of her ever going back there. Even though, in this moment, the old familiar voice was cajoling her, trying to convince her that not only was an occasion like this just a one-time only thing, but that in fact it was the sensible thing to do. Everyone knew brandy was the cure for shock. But the voice of reason, true reason, her reason, was stronger now; visions from the past flickered in her mind's eye, things she'd said, things she'd done, things she'd not done that she should have, appeared like a map of zigzagged routes from bog to mountaintop to bog, and all along the way was lined with ruin. She wouldn't lie; there had been great times, too, moments of bliss and abandon and devastating wit. But oh, the rubble. And now that she knew what it took to get sober she really didn't want to have to do it again. She watched as Sarah made two cups of tea and gave the bottle of brandy back to Jocelyn, asking her to put it out of reach. Jocelyn wished she could tell her it was that easy.

"God, I wish there was something to wear besides this blanket," she said. "I hate wool next to my skin. It's so irritating."

"You're just jealous of my outfit," Sarah said, doing a little pirouette in her handyman's overalls. The men's pants were still hanging from each end of the mantle but only one side of each pair was somewhat dry and anyway they were caked in mud.

"There's chefs' trousers and jackets in the staff room off the kitchen," Karenza said, uttering her first words since they'd come back to the lounge. "And you might even find a couple of the gardener's jackets in there, too."

"Oh, that would be so great," Jocelyn said, beaming at Karenza. And then giving her a quizzical look, she said, "Wait a minute, how come you didn't give that stuff to the guys when they came in soaked?"

"I never miss an opportunity to humiliate men," she whispered.

"That's understandable," Jocelyn said, stroking Karenza's hair.

"Maybe," Karenza said. "But getting even isn't the same as fighting for equality, is it?"

"Maybe in your case it was a necessary first step," Jocelyn said.

Karenza looked at Jocelyn, tears slipping down her cheeks, "I'm so tired," she said.

"Let yourself sleep, we're here."

Sarah offered to go to the staff room while Jocelyn stayed with Karenza. She returned within minutes a look of triumph on her face. "Ta-da," she sang, dumping her haul on one of the armchairs; two pairs of black-and-white checked pants and two classic chefs' jackets of thick white double-breasted cotton which, in spite of many bleachings, sported the remains of various sauce stains; one Cornish fisherman's sweater in heavy charcoal wool with holes at the elbows, and an ancient tweed jacket frayed at the cuffs. She'd also brought one of the oven's racks, which she stood up in front of the fire, hanging Jocelyn and Karenza's underwear and socks from the bars.

"What a brilliant idea," Jocelyn said, wondering if her boots would still be where she'd left them or if, when dawn came, if dawn came, they would have been washed away.

Karenza declined Sarah's offer to help her get dressed, saying she felt strong enough to do it herself. Both she and Jocelyn were grateful that while the chef may have thought himself a giant in the kitchen, in the real world he was a slim, five feet seven inches, so that, while not exactly making a fashion statement, their new outfits fitted fairly well. Once attired, Karenza snuggled back under the blankets with Jocelyn perched on the edge of the mattress, as close to the heat of the fire as she could get while still being able to hold Karenza's hand.

"What should we do about the others?" Sarah asked.

"Where are they?" Karenza asked.

"I'm not sure." There was a brief pause before Sarah groaned, "Oh, my God . . . I hope they haven't gone to the bar room!"

Jocelyn started laughing as she remembered the bowl of vomit on the bar.

"It's not funny," Sarah said, shame making its habitual appearance as the all-encompassing robe that announced her every disgrace.

"Oh, don't go there, Sarah," Jocelyn warned. "Blame it on the roast beef."

"Seriously though," Karenza said, "wouldn't you have loved to have seen their faces when they opened the door?" And the three of them surrendered to a fit of giggles.

It was Sarah who broached the subject again, "We can't leave them out in the cold though, can we?" she asked.

"I know you'd rather it was just us, Karenza," Jocelyn said, squeezing her hand, "But these three men are not the enemy. . . ."

"Even Tom?" Karenza whispered.

"Yes, even Tom. I don't know what his story is, but he strikes me as being deeply wounded."

"He's got a funny way of showing it," Karenza said.

"Come on, Karenza, you of all people know what it's like to have to put on a front."

Karenza started to cry, "But I don't want them to see me."

"Fine. Snuggle under the blankets. Pretend you're asleep if you want. You never know, give them a chance and they might even show you some compassion. If you're ever going to move on, you're going to have to accept that not all men are twisted."

When Karenza conceded, Sarah trotted off to find the men. Something that Jocelyn had just said to Karenza struck a chord with her, too. The shame she had experienced most of her life was not solely attributable to her father's disgrace. She also felt shame for the way she had punished Kenneth, and until she actually dealt with the pain her father had caused her, there would be a never-ending tributary that fed into the river of her shame. The piper, she knew, would come a-calling until he got paid. What she glimpsed through a break in the cycle of shame was the possibility that if she paid him, she could change the tune.

Nonetheless, as she edged towards the bar room she had to struggle with the urge to flee. She searched for an option but, with the possible exception of hiding in a freezing bedroom, found none and so trudged forward.

As soon as she opened the door she realized there was no way they would have stayed in there. Gagging, she closed it quickly and stood in the hallway agonised. How could she possibly face them? She imagined what Kenneth must have felt if they'd gone in there. But maybe they hadn't. Then it finally dawned on her that they must have already known something dire had happened earlier or why would she have left the lounge in a skirt and twin set and returned in handyman's overalls? How long ago had that been? And why had none of them asked her what had happened? Why had Kenneth not taken the opportunity to further humiliate her? Or, if not him, why had Tom passed up such an invitation for sarcastic inquiry? Could it actually have been an act of kindness on their part? Civility. How ironic.

So where had they gone? Obviously nowhere downstairs. She groped her way back down the hall to reception, took a breath and clinging to the banister, slowly made her way upstairs calling out in a voice as cheery as a tea lady's "Yoo-hoo!" When she reached the landing, she heard Charles's voice, a chuckle from Kenneth and then a snort from Tom. Instantly she assumed they must be laughing at her. Although Sarah was used to feeling the urge to flee, she couldn't remember ever feeling the impulse so many times in so short a period as she had tonight. As she turned to leave, the door opened and, even though he was wearing an ankle-length candlewick skirt, she saw that it was her husband.

"Is that you, Sarah?

"Yes," she said. "I was looking for you."

"What's going on?" he asked.

Before she could answer, Tom yelled, "Hey, either come in or go out but close the bloody door."

"Why don't you come in?" Kenneth said and ushered her in.

It was amazing, she thought, how adjusted to the dark one could become, and how, in the dark it was sometimes easier to see what was in front of you than when in broad daylight, even if it was hardly what one expected to see; like Charles and Tom snuggled in bed together and Kenneth getting back in with them and patting the covers for her to join them. An involuntary peal of laughter flew out of her. She laughed until the tears rolled down her cheeks. She laughed until the men laughed with her, all of them able to see the scene as if it were something from a West End farce.

"Goldilocks and the Three Bears," said Charles, and they were off again, Sarah crossing her legs, determined not to wet herself twice in one night. When they finally settled down Kenneth asked her to bring them up to date. Declining Charles' offer to join them under the covers she instead took the spare blanket from the wardrobe, wrapped herself in it and sat on the bed as if to tell a bedtime story.

"She's OK, but she's a bit fragile. And I think she's feeling a bit self-conscious about seeing you all again. So it's probably best to just leave her alone, let her doze and carry on as normal."

"Normal," Tom exclaimed. "What the hell is normal about anything that's happened tonight?"

"Well, yes, but you know, just act as natural as possible, make some tea. . . ."

"Jesus Christ," Charles said. "Maybe we could talk about the weather, too. You're all so fucking British. A young girl has just told us her father is in jail, that the bastard raped her. She nearly jumped off a fucking cliff and we're going to make a cup of tea and act natural? What's natural about being raped by your father? So, what? We all pretend it didn't happen, just sort of wait for it to pass and hope the bridge gets fixed real soon so we can get the hell out of here and good luck to everyone? Unbelievable. No wonder you Brits are such great actors. Not only do you have tons of practice at faking it, you've got thousands of years of repressed feelings at your fingertips. Gives legitimate theatre a whole new meaning doesn't it? It's like the stage is the only legitimate place to let it all out."

"Well, what are we supposed to do?" Tom asked. "Conduct a therapy session in front of the fire? You want to play shrink, go ahead."

"Maybe," Charles said, "something between total avoidance and trying to make it all better would be worth a try."

Listening to them, Sarah picked up on the anxiety they all clearly felt at always being seen as the potential enemy. How often had she had that exact same thought: that men were never to be trusted? Like Karenza had said, in many countries, women were seen as creatures to be controlled and manipulated, hidden and abused, even stoned for being raped, or like here, Britain, merely as objects to have the shit beaten out of them by a drunk husband whose football team just lost. In spite of all this being true, she saw, as she never had done before, how difficult it must be for the good men; that they were judged by lots of women before they as much as opened their mouths. For the first time in her life, Sarah felt compassion for the opposite sex.

"Listen," she said. "Why don't we simply take the lead from Karenza? At the moment she's not interested in how you feel or what you think. She just wants to be invisible. That's what would make her feel safe. If we can do that, it would be enough."

How confusing it must be for Karenza, Sarah thought, gathering the blanket around her. To be so beautiful, so clever, to want to be centre stage but at the same time scared that if you were you might pay for it. How did *she* want to be seen? Certainly not the way she had been tonight. But now that she'd disgraced herself with spiteful revelations and wet knickers, now that she'd been seen at her worst, maybe she could emerge as someone capable of being counted on at the last moment.

Charles had been looking at her, surprised to see a new side of Sarah emerging, and as if reading her mind said, "You know what, Sarah, you may not be capable of hitting the ball out of the park, but you've managed to get three men on base."

37

....

"Before 'lounge re-entry,'" as Charles was now calling it, "shouldn't we be getting more wood and supplies? There's nothing else to do, so we may as well eat!" They explored the dark interior of the fridge, the absence of a light going on when the door opened being another of those shocking little reminders that they really were without power. However, between a bit of groping and their newly acquired night vision, they were able to find a dozen eggs, butter and milk. Sarah also grabbed some frozen peas to use as an ice pack for Charles's hand. And Tom took a frying pan from the rack over the stove while Charles, having spotted a crock of utensils next to it, suggested a wooden spoon might come in handy. Newly swagged, the troupe traipsed back to the lounge.

Jocelyn looked up as they entered and was surprised by a surge of emotion. She beamed at them. How amazing, that these disparate souls had come to represent some sort of solidarity and safety. There was something about their little group that reminded her of AA meetings. Although she had found the dogma a little self-righteous, at its core there was an element of acceptance and witnessing that was its most healing quality. That one could sit in a room full of strangers and reveal one's fears and faults and be neither thrown out nor have anyone walk out, was an experience that over time melted shame right off you. And looking at the little troupe, in their ridiculous outfits, carrying sustenance back to the cave, she felt that some acceptance and witnessing had been evidenced there in the last few hours. They were all powerless, but they were equal in that. Tom stepped carefully around Karenza and put the logs down as quietly as possible. He was about to add more wood to the fire, but Sarah asked if he could just leave it for a while, that it would be easier to scramble the eggs over the embers.

"Good idea," he whispered and turned to steal a look at Karenza. Her still damp hair had fallen in tight curls over her eyes, leaving only her right cheek visible. She looked so young, so tender. He had the impulse to stroke it, actually began to reach for her and then, afraid of frightening her, stepped away.

Now that she had warmed up, Jocelyn had moved to the other side of the mattress, away from the fire, so that she could be equally close to both Karenza and Charles, one hand on Karenza's back, the other reaching for Charles.

Kenneth had angled the couch a little to make room for Sarah's chair, which now formed part of the semi-circle. "So what are we going to eat the eggs with?" Kenneth asked. "Oh bugger," Sarah said, "I forgot forks."

"We don't have plates either," Tom said.

"It's all in the dining room," Karenza whispered, her voice so tiny it took a moment for everyone to register it.

"Why didn't we think of that?" Charles asked, feeling rather proud of having acted so naturally.

"Because you're congenitally stupid," Karenza said, but in a tone so different from the caustic one that had been her default mode before, that everyone knew it was okay to laugh.

"I'll go," Kenneth said.

"I'll help," said Tom, glad to have something to do right now. Sarah put the eggs gently down on the hearth and sat on the floor next to Karenza. "It's just me," she said, giving Karenza's feet a rub. "How are you feeling?"

"Well, you know. A bit in pieces."

Jocelyn stroked her cheek, "Let us be the glue then," she said, and felt Charles's hand on her shoulder. She turned and looked at him and realized they were old enough to be Karenza's parents. Then she looked across at Sarah. In spite of everything she'd gone through that evening, she looked cleansed. Vomiting had helped for sure, but something else seemed to have gone through her. Where there had always seemed to be a blank quality to her face, there was now a softness, yet at the same time, her features seemed to have come forward, as if what had formerly been an ephemeral moon had been humanized with a face that was benign but not anonymous. When Sarah noticed that Jocelyn was looking at her she flushed. But then she saw *how* Jocelyn was looking at her and started to smile, the two of them connecting as equals for the first time in the thirty years they'd known each other.

Kenneth and Tom returned and Kenneth started towards the fire but stopped abruptly. "Um, Karenza?" he asked tentatively. "Is it OK if I come to the fire to make toast?" Jocelyn gave him a thumbs-up sign.

"Yes," Karenza murmured, still not moving.

Sarah and Kenneth worked together in a harmony and rhythm that was wordless and new. Jocelyn watched them. She fantasized how it would be if she and Charles actually were Karenza's surrogate parents, with Sarah and Kenneth her surrogate aunt and uncle. They could create a little family unit that could benefit each of them in different ways. And even though Karenza still hadn't moved, Jocelyn was sure she felt safe with the four of them. But Tom? Where did he belong? Had he ever belonged anywhere? The atmosphere of loneliness emanating from him was palpable, and yet she had no idea how to reach out to him. She turned to him, "How are you doing over there, Tom?"

He looked stricken as he continued to stare at the fire. "I'm all right?" he said. And then, "Actually, no I'm not. Not really." He turned to Karenza, even though from where he was sitting he could only see the outline of her body, which was still in the fetal position.

"Karenza," he whispered, "I'm so sorry."

The silence that followed was potent. Had a man ever apologized to her before? She didn't think so. She knew that he was sorry for how he'd treated her as well as being sorry about her father. And, although she wasn't ready to be seen, she felt her body relax. Felt that she was safe here. She started to weep softly and with the tears came the realization that to reach this feeling of being equal, like so much in life, one had to start with the small things. Sure it was important to fight on the big stage, but it wasn't only about passing laws, or staging demands, was it? It was just as much about quiet acts of courage, or as she'd once heard someone say, giving to those you least wanted to give to. Maybe she'd learned tonight that equality required a combination of kindness and honesty, or as Kenneth would have it, civility and truth. And what better time to start practicing the small gestures than now? She would have liked to reach out from under the covers and hold Tom's hand but she just couldn't do it. She felt the hardness rise up in her, the toughness she used to defend herself. But now the hardness felt like the very thing that would shatter her.

She felt Jocelyn squeeze her shoulder, not the squeeze of comfort, but of encouragement. The words formed in her mind so easily, but the journey from there to the spoken word seemed to take an eternity.

"Thank you, Tom," she said, and uncurled her body just a fraction.

38

No one could remember hearing the grandfather clock issue the hour, but as all three men were wearing watches, it was simple enough to establish that it was now a little after four o'clock.

Jocelyn thought it interesting that none of the women wore watches. She hated them. In her twenties she'd worn one but only as a fashion accessory. She'd rarely looked at it for the time, just to admire the way in which it cohabitated with a wristful of bangles. When drinking, which was an around the clock affair, she hadn't needed a timepiece and even now, although she taught three days a week, she could rely on her body clock to get up early, minus a hangover, and had only to look at the classroom clock or heed the restlessness of certain students to know that the end of a period was nigh.

But men, it seemed, were strapped to time as much as it was strapped to them. Especially men like these three, whether like Charles and Tom, they needed to be continually keeping an eye on the next appointment, or, as in Kenneth's case, had been regimented by army time for so long that checking and double-checking his watch was part of his DNA. And how curious that something as incapable of interpretation as time still could be displayed in such a variety of ways, all of which revealed something about the men who wore them; from Tom's up-to-the-minute luxury Rolex, to Kenneth's faithful old Timex, the traditional middle-class twenty-first birthday gift for boys of his generation upon becoming men, a gift that seemed to take as much as it gave. For along with the importance of the manhood that it so proudly bestowed came also the inescapable fact that time was the marker by which they could now watch their adult lives fly past.

Charles wore a Laco Bauhaus from the forties. Jocelyn's attempt at replacing it was the biggest mistake she'd made in their first year together. She'd never liked its black face, and thinking that she was enlightening him, so to speak, that Christmas she had presented him with a lovely Seiko, an elegant piece with a pale, handsome face, which she had jokingly pointed out was a perfect description of the man himself. He'd been horrified, his own face paling even more as he opened the box. The only thing that had saved her from possible early elimination was the fact that she hadn't known that the one he wore had been his father's.

The wind had picked up again, but the rain was easing off, yet who could tell if it would soon stop or if this was just another tease from nature; a mere respite on the part of the rain, as if stepping aside to let the wind have the spotlight for a while.

After everthing that had happened, it was lovely to see Kenneth and Sarah working together. Even though they weren't addressing each other verbally, it was as though they had each found some solace in cooking together, and with that even, perhaps, a flutter of hope. But, as they say, between hope and expectation lies disappointment, the latter of which Kenneth had lived with all these years.

Tom felt now, much as he had earlier, like the clichéd fifth wheel. Not that he should be surprised by that. He had always been a little aloof. It was his way of staying in control, of making sure that he didn't get hurt again as he had been as a child. Most of the time he managed to elevate himself from being the spare, kept in the trunk, for when one of the others needed replacing, feeling more like the wheel of a unicycle whose jerky back and forth pedaling kept him aloft for no particular reason other than to say, "look, no hands." He felt as if his whole life had been an act performed at altitude, balancing between the drive to go forward while remaining above it all, and the backward pull that threatened to topple him into the repetition of history. But here, in this room, with its seductive glow of fire and candlelight and coupledom he felt himself teetering. Without thinking, he did what he always did when the threat of falling into the void arose; he focused on regaining control by being assertive.

"Right then," he said. "It's time for round five." Even as he said it, he hoped that it would be his turn so that he could finally strut his stuff.

"Do we really want to go on with this?" Charles asked. "It might be uncomfortable for Karenza."

"That's OK," Karenza murmured. No longer in the fetal position, her legs were now almost fully extended, her left leg, bent at the knee, resting on her right leg, in an almost casual position of ease. "Besides," she said, "I want to know what's left to believe in."

Jocelyn got up, stepped over her and took the vase from mantlepiece. Then, crouching in front of Karenza said, "Here, you choose."

Karenza extended a hand, found the two pieces of paper in the bottom of the vase and much like picking Scrabble letters, waited for the piece that "felt" like what she needed. Then, pulling the blanket from her face, she pushed the hair out of her eyes, opened the piece of paper and, looking right at Jocelyn said, "Love."

> PART V <

39

....

Love. There it was.

"Oh really!" Tom groaned. "That's just so ... so flabby." At least there had been something to argue about in the previous rounds, but love was neither a philosophy nor a science. It was an ephemeral cliché. Love had no solidity. Love was a feeling, not a fact, unless you were playing tennis and then it meant zip.

"So I guess we can assume that's not yours then," said Charles with a grin. "But look at it this way, at last we've got something positive to talk about!" He glanced up at Jocelyn taking a reading on her mood, and as the briefest of smiles faded from her lips, a little shiver of danger went through him. This was typical of Jocelyn, to go for something impulsive and straight from the heart. And he noticed that Karenza was still clutching the piece of paper to her chest, as if the love she had been shown in the last hour might disappear as suddenly as it had arrived.

"Away you go then, Jocelyn," Tom said, with a note of sarcasm in his voice. "You reckon spreading a little love is going to be what the new millennium is all about?" Jocelyn glared at him as she got up from the floor and perched on the couch close to Charles as if to get nearer the source.

"You can be cynical if you like, but I believe love is a feeling of deep connection," she said. "And yes, I do think connecting with people is going to be hugely important in the next century. What's the point of any of it if you can't experience deep affection for others? It's about acceptance, too. You know, loving someone warts and all," she stroked Charles's arm.

"Not that I've got any warts you understand . . ." Charles seemed determined to keep it light.

"Course not, darling! Naturally, you are perfect. But you know what, true love goes way beyond all the physical stuff in the beginning. It's more about commitment and loyalty, honesty, forgiveness, compassion. Don't you think these are good things to have more of in our society?" Maybe she was right, but the continuing look of distaste on Tom's face suggested that he was yet to be convinced.

"I know this sounds like a cliché but I do think it starts with loving yourself, "Jocelyn went on. "Mind you, it helps if you have felt loved too."

"Please . . ." Tom was evidently uncomfortable with all this.

"You know, Tom. You're just underlining the problem by being like this. Isn't love what everybody wants? And aren't we all terrified of it? Terrified we can't do it properly, that we're not worthy of it, terrified no one will love us, or if they do, not in the way we want it? Never mind how terrified we all are of losing love. Who wants to set themselves up for grief, how can we survive that?" She looked at Tom and seeing she'd hit his sore spot tried to move love in a different direction. "In the end I think it's about the ability to compromise for the greater good, to be willing to make certain sacrifices, especially when it comes to our children." She paused for a minute, searching for something she felt she had missed.

"And how did you do in that department?" Tom asked, not realizing he had gained himself entry into a game he perhaps didn't want to play.

Jocelyn had clearly been riding high; she had talked passionately in the way someone does who knows their subject so well that they can expound upon it with confidence and certainty. Yet with a single, unwitting blow, Tom had punched the air right out of her. He watched as the passion left her face and was replaced with such anguish that he had to grit his teeth in order to keep looking at her.

She looked away, struggling with emotion. "That was a bit below the belt," she said quietly. "But if you must know, I failed."

"Come on now, darling." Charles said. He tried to reach for her, but she shied away like a shamed animal, sitting as far from him as possible.

"It's OK. Just leave it," she said, and stared into her lap as though by distancing herself she could contain the pain, and prevent it spreading. She was conscious that everyone was looking at her, with the exception of Karenza, who still hadn't moved.

"Look," Charles said gently. "Imperfection comes with parenting, nobody gets it a hundred percent right."

"A hundred percent?" Jocelyn said her voice loaded with sarcasm. "I'd be lucky if I scored ten percent."

"Yes, but you did the best you could at the time," Charles said.

"But it wasn't good enough," she snapped. "*I* wasn't good enough. Sure, I managed not to drink or smoke for nine months. Maybe she'll thank me for that one day. At least I loved her enough not to damage her *before* she was born. No, I waited until she arrived before I started fucking her up." Facing the room now, Jocelyn spoke in a low, bitter tone

"My daughter never knew safety—just like Karenza. I chucked her back and forth between her father and me, moving from place to place, leaving her with babysitters I'd never met, so I could go out dancing and drinking and getting laid. Sure, I always managed to make it look good on the outside, dressing her in groovy outfits, sending her to ballet classes, bringing her to the jazz club while I waitressed as though that was so hip, so cool. Me, the hip mother with her beautiful little daughter, look what a creative, adventurous mother I am, bet you wish *you* could be like that with *your* kid.

And all her little friends thought I was so much fun letting them play with my paints and dress up in my clothes: 'Oh, Mimi's mother listens to Prince and Madonna, Mimi's mother let's her wear lip gloss . . .' Eight years old and I was dressing her like MTV. And you know what? I never chose her over a drink or a man." She crossed her legs, and began kicking one of them back and forth. "You think maybe that's why she hated me by the time she was fifteen? You think maybe that's why she doesn't give a fuck about anybody but herself? You think that's why she tells me it's too late now for me to make it right? Yes, I loved her, I did. I felt love for her, but I didn't do what it takes for a child to *feel* loved. I just called it love. I said the words. I meant them. But it isn't the real thing, is it? You know what? It scared the shit out of me, okay? I had no fucking idea how to be a mother. I had two fucking mothers; one who had no intention, ever, of actually *being* my mother and the other one who tried to be my mother by doing the right thing and calling it love. You know what my mother saw when she looked at me? She saw her husband fucking her sister. I was her fucking martyrdom. As for my so-called *real* mother, what a joke, I was just a moment of sin in her narcissistic life. I don't even know where she is or what happened to her . . ." She was crying now. "I'd do anything to be close with my daughter, but now, when I'm finally capable of being a good mother, she doesn't want me. I've tried. I've tried to make amends with her, but so what. She's right. It *is* too late. I can never, ever go back and make it right. We can never have that time back. No matter what happens in the future I will always have to live with what I did. And I'll carry that shame and regret and sadness with me until the day I die."

Jocelyn went to get up, to flee, but Karenza's hand suddenly wrapped around her ankle. "Don't go," she whispered. "Please don't go." And it was as though the echo of Mimi's voice was right there in the room. How many times had the child begged her, "Don't go, Mama, please don't go"? And yet she always had.

The fear of being needed by her child equal to the need to escape, to run towards what she herself had needed, to be held, to be told everything she'd never felt or believed; that she was the best, that she was desired, that someone loved her like they'd never loved before, that they'd never let her go. That's why she wanted to marry Charles, that's why she longed for him to want that too, she wanted to love and be loved even unto death.

A candle guttered and was gone. Sarah busied herself, lighting each new candle from the old, using a wetted forefinger and thumb to extinguish the old flame before setting the new candle into the warm wax of the old stub.

She'd done her share of judging Jocelyn as a parent over the years but who was she to think she would have been a perfect mother? For the first time in her adult life it occurred to her that along with the sadness of being denied motherhood, came liberation from its burden of inevitable mistakes. And now she wondered: Had she ever been shown love? She scanned her childhood and felt nothing beyond parental maintenance. The boy in the dewy meadow; had that been love? If it had, it certainly hadn't registered. Kenneth? Did loyalty count as love? In thirty years Kenneth had never actually told her he loved her. She'd never heard the words that everyone who loves another longs to hear, "I love you." Even his birthday and Christmas cards to her were signed only with his name. And when had she stopped telling him she loved him? And for how many years had she said "I love you" because she thought if she said it enough times he'd eventually say it, too?

"You know," Charles said, "we all, all of us who are parents, like to think we'll do a better job than our own did. But few of us do. I failed, too, Jocelyn. I know you don't think so, but I did. I never stood up for Jake, really, not with his mother. She automatically got custody and I told myself that's how it should be, a child should be with his mother. But if I'm honest I didn't really want the responsibility, even though deep down I felt he should be with me. You at least stayed with Mimi, you may not have been present in lots of ways but you were there over the long haul and for sure you're there for her now."

"Yes, but she doesn't want me now."

"Oh, yes she does. She doesn't know it because she's too busy getting even, or she thinks she is. But she's an adult now. Now it's her turn to take responsibility for her life, just like you're taking responsibility for yours. It's what I've always loved about you, your willingness to stop blaming everything on those who hurt you as a child. Shit, none of us really want to grow up. We all want to be taken care of, don't we? Especially in the way that we feel we weren't as kids. Who was the writer who said anyone who had a childhood has a story to tell? But that's all it is; once it's in the past it's just a story we tell and the more invested we become in it, the more we embellish it in order to excuse our behaviour, the more we become a slave to it." He was quiet for a moment, as he allowed his own words to reveal what he'd never seen before. "In fact, d'you know what I think?" he said. "I think I used my father's suicide to justify my own absence as a father. The pain I felt when my father killed himself, not to mention the guilt, was so overwhelming I was determined never to hurt my son like that. Better not to get too attached to him, better for him not to get too close and then feel bad if something happened to me. But the truth is, I was afraid of being a father. You'd think having a father who stuck with me through everything, until he didn't, you'd think I'd know how to do that. But it's almost like the manner of his death robbed me of all the love he'd shown me. As if, with that one act, he revealed that it had been a sham all along. Because if he loved me, really loved me, he would never have killed himself. His act made a mockery of love. It made everything we'd felt for each other, everything we'd shared, seem like a lie."

He paused again, looking towards the fire as if in its warmth he could rekindle what had been lost. "I feel love," he said quietly. "I feel love for my son and for you, Jocelyn, but I have a hard time trusting it. Like you said, one way or another love carries loss in its heart. Is it any wonder I put so much store by impermanence?"

40

The fire was now so hot it was difficult to get close to it. Even Karenza, although not turning away from it, pushed the covers down from her face and neck. She had watched Tom as he tended it earlier, admiring his quiet, easy capability, a capability that maybe extended beyond the boundary of his lonely heart.

Jocelyn, having now turned to Charles, took his good hand and kissed the palm before holding it to her cheek, hoping to convey to him how much it meant to her, what he'd just shared. Seeing that the bag of peas had slipped from his hand, she picked it up to replace it and felt that it had thawed and as such was useless. She stood up to take it to the sideboard and felt Karenza's hand tighten around her ankle. She reached down and touched her, "I'll be right back," she said.

She put the peas on one of the dirty plates on the sideboard and stood for a moment looking at the other five, all of them watching the fire. All of them apparently isolated in various stages of thaw, with the exception of Tom, who seemed frozen at the core and intent on remaining that way. She walked back to the couch and as she passed him gently caressed his shoulder, feeling him wince. Sitting on the edge of the couch she bent over Karenza and whispered, "I'm back," instinctively stroking the girl's head and felt the joy of having her touch received.

"Well," she said, "now that Charles and I have revealed how inadequately we've loved our children does anyone else have any thoughts on the subject?"

"This whole business of love," Kenneth said, as if thinking aloud, "it completely confuses me. I've been sitting here thinking what does love mean to me and I have absolutely no idea. Not when it comes to people. I loved going for bike rides when I was a boy. Loved leaving our house, even before Dad did what he did, because the house was so … joyless. It wasn't that our parents hated each other, they just didn't love each other, at least not that I could see. There was no warmth was there?" he said, glancing at Jocelyn. "Not until you came along." And, turning back to the fire, "So I'd get on my bike and sail out into the country. I loved being self-sufficient. I used to prop my bike against a stone bridge to eat an apple and watch the water rushing under it, you know, trying to follow a single rivulet. And I loved making my model aeroplanes and all that. But when it comes to people, I don't know what it means. Isn't love meant to be shared? I think I'm missing that gene."

No one was looking at anyone. The discomfort in the room was paralyzing, and yet Kenneth seemed to have no idea of the effect he was having on the others.

"And then," he continued, "When you add sex to it … well …" his eyebrows raised in a sort of resigned amazement, "*That* I find utterly confusing. Did my father love Aunt Jean? I don't think so. She certainly didn't love him. She didn't love anything or anyone I don't think. Did our mother love you, Jocelyn?" he asked, without turning to her. "Or was she just doing the right thing? I don't know, maybe she took you in to punish him." He grabbed the poker and moved a piece of wood to the back of the grate. "Actually," he said, "you were the first person I loved and felt loved by." Of course in his English way, Kenneth couldn't quite manage to look at Jocelyn as he said this, but he went on. "This was particularly confusing to me because I hated you before you were born. I hated you so much I'd already made up my mind to leave home as soon as I could. But mum and dad wouldn't let me join the army until I was twenty." He turned towards Jocelyn.

"I remember Mum bringing you home, you know. Dad was on a business trip and she brought you into the front room and you were so tiny and so perfect and so you, with your little thatch of auburn hair and Mum put you in my arms and for the first time I felt love for someone. You looked at me, the way you still do, so directly. I wanted to stay and protect you until you were grown-up but I couldn't stand being in the house with Dad. And this is what confuses me," he said, looking at Jocelyn now, his face pinched between pain and fury, "if love is so all-fucking powerful, why did I leave you?"

"Oh, Ken, dearest Ken," Jocelyn said. "You were twenty. You were tormented. You'd seen our father. . . ."

"Don't!" he shouted. Sarah looked stunned, presumably wondering where the hell she fitted into all this.

"Are you saying," Tom asked, "that your only experience of love started with bike-riding and ended with your baby sister?"

The heat of the room seemed pitched against the world beyond the window, as if it were the last burning ember in the centre of a dark universe.

"Not exactly. I loved a girl once," Kenneth said, his voice now a faint lament as he told the story of that day on the beach with Suzanna. When he finished, he looked down at his lap and saw his hands lying there like old gloves, gloves he'd worn his whole life to protect him from human touch. He watched as one of them left the other and hovered for a moment before making the long journey to Sarah's lap, felt his hand taking hers, felt, actually felt, his fingers wrap around hers, felt how small and vulnerable they were and whispered the words Sarah had wanted to hear perhaps as much as she wanted to hear "I love you" . . . "I'm sorry," Kenneth said, "I'm so sorry."

Sarah felt a leg cramp beginning, but chose to suffer it rather than withdraw her hand from Kenneth's. This was like being on a first date; his skin around her skin. She wanted to squeeze his hand but was afraid that if she did he would take it as a sign to let go and so she didn't move, barely breathed, and then worried if maybe she felt lifeless to him, became afraid of being misread as usual and what could be done about that? She leaned towards him and whispered, "Thank you."

The room was pulsing, as though if anybody moved the spell would be broken. Jocelyn looked at Kenneth and Sarah—perhaps there was hope for them. But this was a heightened moment, in this place, in this situation, which, once it took on an air of disbelief could, as with every expansion, result in a contraction. Jocelyn really couldn't hold it in any longer, "I absolutely have to go to the toilet," she said.

"Me too," Charles said.

"Nobody move," Jocelyn said, "I don't want to miss anything."

Although she was partly jesting, Tom and Karenza were happy to take it as an order, while Sarah and Kenneth were experiencing a shared silence that for now said more than they were otherwise capable of expressing.

Jocelyn and Charles made their way upstairs to one of the spare bathrooms.

"Keep me company," Jocelyn said, as she sat on the toilet. He stood listening to her pee and thought he had never loved her more. Hoped that he'd be able to keep her company until they were incontinent. When she was finished she unzipped him and watched as he held his penis with the good hand, while keeping the injured one up to his chest, the arm bent at the elbow.

"You need a sling," she said, as he shook his penis.

"It's not *that* big," he said, and they both cracked up.

"Seriously, though," Jocelyn said, when she finally caught her breath.

"You can't hold your arm up like that. Maybe I can find a tea towel in the kitchen." She gave him a playful squeeze as she zipped him back up. He kissed the top of her head and she brought her mouth up to his and lingered there with him, neither of them looking for more than the familiarity of each other and, finding it, the rare moment of love's simplicity.

When they returned to the lounge, having successfully found a tea towel, it was like entering a game of freeze. Nobody seemed to have changed position and for a moment Jocelyn though she might have to yell, "move." Instead, following Charles' instructions, she made a sling for him.

"How's that feel?" she asked.

"Much better. Now I can sit up and join the party."

Jocelyn reached down and touched Karenza. "How are you doing?" she asked.

"I'm hungry."

"Can I make you scrambled eggs on toast?" Sarah asked.

"Yes, please."

Kenneth went to the sideboard to get her a plate and fork. Tom still seemed frozen.

"It's an interesting subject, isn't it, love?" Charles said, to no one in particular. "You'd think, seeing as everyone wants it, that it would be easy."

"Yes," Jocelyn said. "But wanting something and believing in it are two different things."

Without looking at anyone, Karenza slowly sat up and, swinging her legs toward the fire, rested her back against the couch. She looked briefly at Sarah as she thanked her and began to eat, her hand shaking so much that the first forkful of eggs fell back to the plate. She finally managed to load up a slice of toast, folded it over and took a bite. Sarah poured her some tea and urged her to drink, thinking how good it felt to give and have it received. Why had she not thought of reaching out to someone before tonight when there were so many people in need of love? Karenza finished the last mouthful of egg on toast. "That was really good," she said, giving the empty plate to Sarah. "My mum used to make me scrambled eggs on toast when I was ill," she said. "I'm supposed to be looking after her now. I feel bad that I'm not with her."

"Is she still bedridden?" Charles asked, the question so simple and natural that it didn't occur to anyone, not even Karenza, that it was the first time since she'd been brought back from the edge, so to speak, that one of the men had spoken directly to her.

"Not anymore," she replied. "But she tires easily and she still has some pain."

"Was the operation a success?" Charles asked.

"I think so. It's only been a couple of weeks but she seems to feel positive about it, but that's mum, always shining it on. You don't ever really know with her."

"Did she know about your father?" Charles asked and immediately felt like he'd put his foot in it. "I'm sorry, I shouldn't have asked. If you don't want to talk about it I completely understand."

"It's okay. Yeah, she knew," Karenza said. "But not for a couple of years. It took me that long to tell her."

"How come?" Jocelyn asked.

"Because my dad said he'd kill me if I told and I believed him. But then when I started my period I was more afraid of getting pregnant than I was of dying, so I finally told her and she threw him out. That's when he started raping other girls." She was quiet for a while, fiddling with her knife and fork before putting her plate back on the hearth.

"I don't understand love either," she continued. "I know my mum loved me, but I don't understand how you can love someone and not know when something bad is happening to them. I don't understand how she couldn't have known what my dad was doing. And I don't understand what happened with them. When my dad left, she burned all the photos of them from when they were young. He'd always said that they were made for each other. But then, when I was born, that was it. No more happy photos. Not one of him holding me. Only one of mum and me, when I was a baby. He said it was all my fault. That mum stopped loving him when I was born. So what's the deal? Does everyone have a quota for love? Like maybe some people can only love one person at a time and others have enough for a whole family? Why do I have to feel guilty that my mum loved me?"

"Only they can know what happened between them," Charles said. "But it was their failure, you weren't responsible for it."

"Yeah, but I had to pay the price."

What could one say? It was inarguable. Who in that room could say otherwise? It didn't matter that the whole family had paid a price, each in their own way; only one of them had been raped. Yet who could say who'd paid the most? Did being violated rank higher than spending your life in jail and having to live with the horror of how much damage you'd inflicted on your child? Did her father even feel remorse or had he so damaged his soul that he still felt he was the victim? How did a man go from loving his young wife to raping his young daughter? And what was that bullshit about going to prison in order to pay your debt to society? His debt wasn't to society, it was to his child and where had society been when his child had needed it?

"You know, Karenza," Charles said, "I totally get what you're saying. But . . ."

"But what?" Karenza asked.

"You could choose not to keep paying."

"What do you mean?" Karenza said, an edge creeping into her voice.

"You could stop believing all men are like your father."

She started to say something but Charles put up his hand, "I'm going out on a limb here, Karenza, because I think you're worth the risk, but do me a kindness, let me finish before you cut me off at the knees." She smiled a little in spite of herself and he continued, "You are a highly intelligent and beautiful young woman, but you're wasting both those gifts. You say you believe in equality but really you're more interested in getting even. Correct me if I'm wrong, but I have the feeling the only equality you're really practicing is in treating all men as the enemy. If you don't pay attention and get some help you'll continue to behave in a way that will always attract the worst in men so that you can prove yourself right. But what are you protecting yourself from, really? There are three imperfect men in this room, but, and of course I can only speak for myself, I see a young woman who has been so profoundly wounded it makes me want to weep. It does not make me want to take advantage of you. I would do anything to help you. But you have to start letting good people in, Karenza. Look around this room and tell me you're not among friends. Tell me that tonight, here in this room, you haven't been given love and respect. Don't squander it."

Karenza was still looking at him.

"You're lucky I'm a wounded man, or I'd be giving you a hug."

She looked at him through tears, "I'll take a raincheck."

41

....

"So Jocelyn," Tom said, but this time without the edge in his voice. "Exactly why do *you* believe in love?"

"Because I feel it," Jocelyn said. "And if I feel it, then it exists."

"That's a bit grandiose, isn't it?" Tom said.

"I meant, for me," Jocelyn said. "If *I* feel something then it exists for *me*."

"So what does it feel like to you?" Tom persisted.

"Good," she said, looking right at him. "It feels good. It feels kind, forgiving, warm, healing. Sometimes it feels so joyous, so exciting it's almost overwhelming, as in, I love you so much I'm going to burst."

"I'm flattered," Tom said.

"Don't be. I most certainly don't feel that way about you. I feel that way about Charles. But with you I feel sad not joyous. I wonder, actually if that's something you ever feel?

"What?"

"Joy."

"My turn for the bathroom," he said, already on his way to the door. He gave her a theatrical wave as he left the room.

"That was a bit harsh, wasn't it?" Charles said, when the door had closed.

"Look," Jocelyn said. "Just because I believe in love doesn't mean I practice it a hundred percent of the time. The man gets under my skin, okay? I know, I know, he's been hurt," she said, rolling her eyes. "Who the hell hasn't?"

"Evidently no one in this room," Karenza said.

Jocelyn looked disturbed now, like she'd ruined something precious that had been happening. As though she'd been caught revealing a side of herself she detested. She knew she was guilty of showing love and compassion only when it came easily, but wasn't the true measure of love attained from loving the people that you judged the most? And what was it about Tom that bothered her so much? If she were younger she would have probably been attracted to him, fallen in love with him, back then when she called need "love," back then when the men who were least emotionally available were the ones she was guaranteed to fall for. But she had Charles now, so what was the big deal? Could it really be as trite as the fact that Tom was as unreachable as her father had been?

She could count on one hand the times that she and her father had connected and all of those times had been before she knew who her real mother was. Of course she recognized that she had been used as a punishment against her father. It had been about duty not love. But where the fuck had *he* been? Was the man spineless? Why hadn't he demanded a ceasefire? So he made a terrible mistake, but no one had forced his wife to take Jocelyn in. Yes, that's what irritated her about Tom; he had the same combination of distance, repressed anger and, in her judgment, cowardice. What had he revealed of his inner self during the course of this night? Yet how quick he was to push everyone else's buttons. A coward and a bully. And yet she had glimpsed in him an agony that had made her long to reach out to him, just as she'd always felt her father's agony.

Jocelyn had been relieved, if she was honest, when her father died. He took with him the focus of her blame and resentment. But then she'd become aware of the hollowness at the core of her relationship with her mother, realized that it had always been there. But she too was dead now. She'd died in her sleep. An unconscious death after a long, unconscious life.

42

....

Tom sat at the desk in his room and looked out to sea. There were still white caps visible even in the dark and enough wind to scrape the ivy against the edge of the window. It set his teeth on edge. As did that Jocelyn woman. God, what a night. Would it never end? He looked at his watch. Four forty-five. Maybe when the sun rose, if it ever did, he'd go down to the bridge and see what the damage was. Maybe the water would have subsided enough to rig a way of crossing the stream. If he remembered correctly it had only been about eight feet wide.

He switched on his phone, looking for a miracle. No service. He opened his computer, which he'd put to sleep before going down to dinner so it was still close to fully charged. The screen almost an obscenity, its harsh rectangle of light making him feel even more disconnected in the dark. It was open to Lily's email, which he'd read a dozen times on the way down on the train and then again before he'd dressed for dinner; each time searching for an opening through which he could either re-enter the relationship or escape the pain of its demise. But the same message lay bare before him. *I'm so sorry, I know you're hurt, but . . .* There was no way to misread her email the way he'd misread her in the flesh . . . she was *fond of him, but . . . he was interesting, but . . . she wished she loved him, but . . . and you know what? . . .* The sentence finished once and for all . . . *you didn't really love me either. We just looked good on paper, but paper is so thin. Love is more than a list of pros and cons. Equality in age and fitness, ambition and achievement, in having a similar aesthetic, the same taste in movies and food . . . that's yuppie love . . . I was never looking to see myself reflected in a man's eyes. I want a man into whose eyes I can disappear . . .* And then the platitudes, the insistence that he'd get over her in no time, the wishing him the best of everything and the killer sign off . . . *fondly, Lily.*

He snapped the computer shut. Love. What a joke. And look at that lot downstairs. What a mess of humanity, all of them with their high-minded, self-righteous beliefs. And look where their beliefs had gotten them. And now love. The cliché of the night. Spare me, he thought. But he had been spared, hadn't he? Where had love existed in his life? His father, like Jocelyn's mother, had done his duty, but love? His father had been too busy loving his mother and look how well that had worked out. Is that how he was going to end up, a sixty-year-old man living alone, dating women half his age? Or would he end up like Kenneth, married to an alcoholic frump? And suddenly, as if watching a film, he saw a young Kenneth running into the sea . . . the girl calling to him and then the screen tears and another film is playing. Tom's young mother is in the sea calling to him, "Come on. Don't be afraid, my love, I'll hold you. Trust me, you'll be safe." And as he wades in a wave comes, he panics but she has him, she's holding him above the water, carrying him farther out beyond the waves and floating him in her arms; she has him. He looks up at her, her eyes bluer than the sky, her dark blonde hair clinging to her neck. He feels her breasts next to his cheek. "Relax," she says. "Let your head go. I have you."

It had been his seventh birthday. His dad was in court all day defending a client. His mother had been in bed the day before with a hangover. Tom had assumed he'd just go to school as usual. Maybe there would be a cake for dinner. But instead his mother had woken him early. He can hear the sound of his bedroom curtains on the rod as she whips them open, can see the morning sun outlining her in gold, sees her face as she turns to him, "We're playing truant today," she says and tickles his feet. "Come on lazy bones."

He has no idea where they went. Has no recollection of how they got there, or the return home. What he remembers now is the feeling of safety in her arms, just the two of them in the enormous sea, the look of love on her face as she looks down at him, the way she towels him dry and then holds him in her arms to warm him. He vaguely remembers fish and chips and screaming gulls, an ice-cream cone dipped in chocolate . . . and then the film ends.

What had Karenza said, something about a quota of love? So that had been his, he thought, a few hours, out of the blue and then gone. The intensity of the love he'd felt between him and his mother was a cruelty etched so deeply that only acid could erase it. Who says it's better to have loved and lost than never to have loved at all. Love, he thought, the one thing you could never count on.

He thought about getting under the covers and staying there, but he knew he'd never sleep and he didn't want the others to think he was skipping out just when it was time for him to have his turn. Besides, if anything could bring this sentimental crap to an end it would be the thing he believed in most. He went down-stairs, stopping in the kitchen to pick up another armful of wood.

Even before he opened the door he could hear laughter and hoped perhaps they were done with love, which as far as he was concerned was no laughing matter.

"What's so funny?" he asked, unloading the wood.

"Oh, it's OK, Tom," Jocelyn said slightly sheepishly, remembering her last comment about him being joyless. "We were all trying to remember quotes about love. So far we've had 'love is blind but marriage is an eye opener'—thank you Ken! And 'if love is blind why is lingerie so important?' And I'm afraid to say that was my dear Charles."

"Good one," Tom said, taking up his seat once more. "Chekhov is my man. I quote, 'If you're afraid of loneliness don't marry.'"

"There you go again," Karenza said. "Why do you have to be so cynical?" She saw the look of incredulity appear on Tom's face. "I know, I know, that's sounds a bit ripe coming from me, but when Jocelyn pulled me back from the edge before, something went out of me. Maybe it was hatred that went over the cliff. I hope so, because I tell you, it takes a lot of energy to hate, and I should know." She looked down at her hands for a moment and then turned to Tom. "It takes a lot of energy," she repeated, "to always be on the lookout for the worst in everyone. And d'you know what else I realized? It's soul-destroying, because you get good at finding the worst in everyone and it ends up that's all you can see. It's lonely out there on the edge of judgment and believe me, I've judged all of you," she paused, giving them all a wicked look. "Mostly we only see people's masks anyway, don't you think?" she continued. "And obviously some people wear masks that are sure to put people off." She paused and looked down at her hands again. "I don't know what I'm saying really."

"Oh, but you do," Jocelyn said. "And you're saying it beautifully. Do you know that line by James Baldwin. Let me see, how does it go?" She thought for a moment, "Right, he said, *love takes off the mask that we fear we cannot live without and know we cannot live within.*"

"Say that again," Karenza said. As Jocelyn repeated it the grandfather clock matched its meter with five measured strokes. Six heads turned toward the window, all hoping to see a glimpse of dawn, but the world still lay in darkness.

43

For once it was Sarah who tentatively broke the silence. "I know you'll probably all think it's corny, but I keep hearing Paul Mc-Cartney singing, *And in the end, the love you take, is equal to the love you make.* I loved that song when it came out. It made so much sense to me, platonically, I mean. I think he meant it that way, don't you?" She sounded flustered but pushed on anyway. "The thing is, even though I believed it, I just didn't know how to get started." She looked at the fire and continued talking as if Kenneth weren't in the room. "I thought that if I kept loving Kenneth that eventually he'd love me, too. But now I don't know if I *was* loving him, or just saying the words. I think I was saying it in the hopes that he'd love me and then I'd be unfrozen or something. Christ, I sound like Sleeping Beauty."

"Don't take the Lord's name in vain, now," Kenneth said, in an attempt at covering up his embarrassment.

"That is *so* typical of you," Sarah turned on him. "I'm trying to say how I feel and you're making fun of me and when you're not making fun of me you just ignore me."

"I'm sorry," Kenneth said. "I'm not trying to make fun of you. I haven't a clue, any more than you, obviously, I mean, not you obviously . . . oh for God's sake. What's the use? I'm too old for this."

"Oh, Ken, snap out of it," Jocelyn said. "Here's the quote for you, *every crisis presents an opportunity.* What a bunch of bawling infants we all are. God knows, I am a demanding bitch."

"Hear, hear," Charles said.

"Pipe down you," she said, smiling at him. "Look, love is bloody hard work, Ken. It's like art, it's not something that happens on its own; you have to show up for it. The trouble is we expect it to be perfect, which basically means a hundred percent love, a hundred percent of the time, or else we're not playing. How ridiculous. And you know what? We're always looking for an out, so we don't have to do the work. Yes, I've still got my running shoes, too." She said, looking at Charles. "There is no perfect bloody love. But each of us can increase the percentages. I've always loved you, Ken, because without you I'd never have experienced love as a child. So I know you're capable of it. What I really feel bad about is Sarah. I've been crap and you've needed so much more. And you're right; the love you take *is* equal to the love you make."

Tom was practically squirming. Maybe going over the cliff wasn't such a bad idea. He didn't know how much more of this he could take.

"You're very quiet, Tom," Charles said. "We haven't heard much from you on the subject of love."

"Nor will you," Tom said. "I don't really believe in it. We've been spouting on about it since year dot and here we are, turn of the millennium and there's more hatred than ever. I think love is an abstract idea that has no basis in reality. Love is a bargaining chip; I'll love you if you give me xyz. Look at the six of us. How much so-called love were we all given as children? Look at the holocaust, look at the religious fanatics. Look at politicians for Christ's sake. And what about all this ethnic cleansing, wow, lot of love there. Or, how about let's club some baby seals, or beat up some queers, or throw battery acid in your Indian girlfriend's face because her dowry isn't big enough. I mean, really, where is the love?"

"But surely you believed in it when you proposed to your girlfriend," Jocelyn interrupted.

"Touché," Tom said. "Actually, I think I thought I believed in it. After all, I am human, who doesn't *want* to believe in it. We all fall in love and live happily ever after. Right? You talk about percentages but the odds of getting love are pretty low aren't they?"

"Surely you must have experienced love in your life, from someone?" she said.

"Yes. Seven hours," he said.

"What do you mean?"

"I experienced seven hours of love one day when I was little. That was my mother's quota. At least she spent it all at once," he said bitterly.

"I'm so sorry," Jocelyn said.

"That's something else I don't believe in," he said. "People say they're sorry and then like good Catholics after confession they go out and do the same thing over and over again. I think love and apology are cheap commodities for which we pay too high a price."

"So, what do you believe in then?" she asked.

"Money."

> PART VI <

44

There was an immediate silence in the room, the kind of silence that descends when an inebriated guest says something hostile at an intimate dinner party; the hostility robbing the evening of all goodwill and replacing it with fear, regret, alienation, embarrassment, resentment and a sadness bordering on desolation. Money; the word itself flung, much like Tom had earlier flung the engagement ring. A hurled obscenity, once again aimed at Jocelyn but ricocheting off her and slapping everyone in the face with its mundane yet spiteful inevitability. Tom's belief, while not really a surprise to anyone, nonetheless removed the last traces of hope that any of them might have held onto; hope that they could all agree that love was the answer; that love would embrace them all, Tom included. Money, even in the abstract, had the power to do what it does in reality; that is to say, it separated them from each other. Put them in their place according to their worth, not as basically good, hardworking people, but their worth according to ambition and achievement; success and failure measured at face value.

Karenza drew the covers up to her chin and stared at the fire, which would soon need more wood. Money had played its role in the demise of her parents' marriage. Even though she didn't want to admit it, it may have been the root cause of what had happened to her. Karenza knew poverty. She knew the humiliation of going with her mother to collect their benefits while her father stood in the unemployment line. She could still feel the heat in her cheeks when a school chum saw her and her brothers scavenging for wood from a skip so they could keep one room of the house warm. Then there were the desolate evenings (after the TV had been repossessed) when her father went to the pub with the grocery money, while her mum made baked beans on stale toast. She'd started earning bits and bobs of cash from an early age, well before she was old enough to start working at The Morvah. And she'd squirreled it away. But she remembered now how her mum had encouraged her to follow her heart, and have a career doing something that really mattered to her. That she shouldn't worry about money, real wealth came from how you lived. Tears welled up as she thought about her mum's guiding voice, even though she had found herself in the grimmest of circumstances.

But she'd had her eyes opened at university. She'd known fellow students in their final year headhunted by banks and financial institutions offering salaries that were hard to turn down by students too young yet to have formed a moral core. Who wanted to work their way through medical school, or the liberal arts, never mind philosophy or the humanities when you could ride the wave of hedge funds and start-ups and maybe get a year-end bonus that was bigger than your parents' combined annual salary? Money, the new pop idol, promising hit after hit after hit.

The chill that now pervaded the room seemed to have nothing to do with a lack of heat but with a sudden lack of heart as if the mere mention of money had taken something vital from their midst and left in its place an absence, much as when one reaches for something familiar and finds it is not in its usual place.

"Well, I must say, it's a bit of a bummer going from love to money," Charles said. "But I'm sure we'd all love to hear why money is the thing you believe in most."

"Well, it's obvious, isn't it?" Tom answered. "It's the one thing everyone absolutely needs in order to live."

"What rubbish. What about food and water? What about breathing?" Karenza said.

"Nice try," Tom replied, "but not well thought out. In order to breathe you have to eat. In order to eat you have to buy food."

"What if you grow your own food?" Karenza said.

"Oh, come on, don't be naïve. Where do you grow it? On land you own or rent, no? For which you need money."

"Well, there are still some tribes, like in the Amazon, where they live completely off the land, without owning it."

"And how much longer do you think that will last?" Tom asked. "Logging companies are already buying and destroying their land. It's just a matter of time. By the end of the first decade of the new millennium money will be an absolute necessity even to those tribes. And where will they go? What will they do to earn money once their land is taken?"

"We may all have agreed that believing in God, any god, is foolish," said Kenneth, throwing another log on the fire, relieved that unlike the coffee he drank, the wood was not from Brazil. "But believing in money, having money as your primary belief seems entirely callous. It's people like you that give birth to sayings like 'money is the root of all evil.' And you don't have to believe in God to believe in evil, do you?"

"Look," Tom said, somewhat defensively. "If I'm going to believe in something then I have to be able to count on it and money is the only thing you can count on."

"Count, or control?" Jocelyn asked.

"Both."

"Well, that's like saying you believe you can control something which is totally abstract." Charles said. "What about fluctuations in currencies, recessions, crashes in the stock market? Since when did the money markets have control of these? I mean, we're all control freaks to some extent, but it's human folly, isn't it? Things go wrong."

"I disagree with you," Tom said. "I think control is about taking responsibility and the majority of people don't want to take responsibility when it comes to money. They don't want to know about it. Why do you think people are more in debt now than ever? Everyone wants what they want, and they want it now and they'll believe anything to get it. Everyone wants to blame the rich guys but the majority of people who are poor are poor because they're stupid or greedy or lazy or a combination of all three."

"What a totally heartless thing to say!" said Jocelyn, plainly furious. "Are you implying that all people have equal opportunity? What about people living in the third world? Are they just stupid and greedy and lazy?"

"You know perfectly well that's not what I'm talking about. But yes, some of those people are stupid, lazy and greedy, too. That's a different conversation. I'm talking about us, Europeans, Americans . . ."

"But it's not just about us Europeans and Americans, is it? What about the rest of the world's populations? That's just pure arrogance," Jocelyn interrupted. "But okay, what about the person who gets laid off right before his pension kicks in, or the person who doesn't have health insurance and not only loses his job when he get seriously ill but also has to spend his life savings on medical expenses?"

"There you are," Tom said, a note of triumph in his voice. "A perfect example of not taking responsibility. Instead of putting all his money into savings, he should have put some into health insurance. But no, he decided to believe he'd never get sick. Not him. He'd retire with all his savings and play golf or whatever for the rest of his life. Money is black and white," he continued. "Either you have enough or you don't." Tom was on his feet now, jangling the small change in his pocket. "If you want to keep your head above water come the new millennium, you'd better wise up, because with the Internet, the whole game is changing. There will be so much more competition popping up and so many more services that everyone can become an investor. Wall Street? The London Stock Exchange? They will be part of cyberspace, virtual reality. People'll be making money off of nonexistent commodities. It's all going to move so fast and become so complicated that if you don't take heed now you'll be sunk by 2010."

"That sounds a bit extreme to me," Kenneth looked unconvinced.

"No, I'm serious. By my reckoning even debts will become commodities for banks to make money from. So, if I have one piece of advice it would be, get out and stay out of debt. And if you don't want to keep up with what's happening in the financial industry, then you'd better have a budget and stick to it."

"But what about me?" Sarah spoke as though she had just been awoken from a trance. "What about someone like me?" Sarah had never earned money of her own. She'd always left all that to Kenneth. She had never been one of those feminists busy fighting for equal pay. But now she felt frightened and needed a drink. Confusion and/or alcohol were vital for warding off fear. When had it happened that the two had become entwined to the point that now without the one, alcohol, the other, confusion, was not quite foolproof? Breathe, that's what Charles had told her she should do when she felt the onset of panic. And so she did, concentrating on a particular flame that was darting in and out of a hole in one of the logs.

The clock struck six and it was like Maxwell's silver hammer, as if with every chime her fear was struck anew until she heard a clear and present thought. She had never grown up. That was it. She didn't want to know about money because she wanted to be taken care of. And she hadn't asked for much, had she? She'd never complained about Kenneth's income and pension. But it had never actually occurred to her that she could have been what they called "upwardly mobile." It had never occurred to her to get a job. Her mother hadn't worked, but then as a vicar's wife bringing up six children that would have been frowned upon. But what was her excuse? How could she have lived to be fifty-six and not only never have earned money but know nothing about it? And now here was this young man steeped in it apparently. It sounded horrifying. What did he mean debt would be the new commodity? What was a commodity? Where would she stand in this new world?

"So," Jocelyn said. "How does it feel to make money off the corporations that make money off other people's misery?"

"Quite smart, actually," Tom replied. "I know you don't think much of me, and obviously you see the world through a different lens than me. But what right do you have to assume that because I don't believe in love I am therefore morally bankrupt? If it weren't for people like me making sure these corporations stay within the law, you've no idea just how incredibly bad things would be."

"Oh, come off it," Jocelyn cried. "They pay you to find ways around the law. 'Loopholes' I believe they're called. So you focus on the minor technicalities while the big boys aim the canons? Not much of a risk taker, are you? The irony is that money is a shield for you."

"What *are* you talking about?" Tom said.

"It protects you from your emotions. You just don't want to go there—it's obvious from tonight. And you seem to have convinced yourself that money is an emotion-free zone where you can just go and exercise your considerable skill as a lawyer. But drop your guard for a moment and someone might rob you. Or, you might feel something? Money is cold-blooded, right? That's why the richest people are often the most ruthless; it's the only option besides being catatonic for those who wish to avoid the messiness of feelings."

A log fell in the grate. She got up, reached for the poker and with one deft move, placed the errant piece at the back of the fire.

"You know what Kenneth said earlier about money being the root of all evil. The saying actually goes: 'For the *love* of money is the root of all evil.' How's that as an equation?"

Her heart was racing and, wanting to dispel the adrenalin of her outburst, she went to the sideboard, asking if anyone wanted anything, while helping herself to a piece of cheese and yet another digestive biscuit.

"God! Is there any Valium over there?" Karenza asked, trying to make light of how unsettled she felt.

She swept aside the blankets and stood up and Charles burst out laughing, just as Kenneth had reached the door on his way to fetch wood. "What's so funny?" he asked.

"Well, look at us," Charles said, "Talk about gender swapping." They looked at each other and started laughing; the men in candlewick, chenille and tartan skirts, the women in chefs' pants and mechanic's overalls. Charles could barely get his breath, "After the heated discussion we've just heard," he said. "It gives a whole new meaning to cross-dressing doesn't it?"

Even Tom eventually melted and joined in the laughter, the planes of his face softening and expanding. Jocelyn looked at him perhaps seeing a glimpse of the boy on the beach.

"What a shame none of us chose laughter as our thing," Sarah said. "It seems to be the one thing that makes us all feel good."

Kenneth, his hand on the doorknob, looked across the room at his wife. The fact that some of that old innocence remained intact in spite of the failure of their marriage and the ruin of her drinking seemed miraculous, not to mention that she, out of all of them, had made this simple observation and delivered it with exquisite timing. For what, indeed, was more universal than laughter? And if laughter was the best medicine, then maybe it was time he and Sarah increased the dosage. She looked up at him and smiled. He smiled back and, with a dramatic swish of candlewick that made her giggle, he left for the kitchen.

45

....

"You OK?" Karenza asked Jocelyn, putting a tentative hand on Jocelyn's leg. "I'm just fine. What about you?"

"I'm OK," she said. "Bit shaky. More disoriented than anything." She paused for a moment, pulling the tweed jacket close across her chest. "I've never done drugs. I never wanted to lose control like that, but I feel like I imagine it would feel to drop acid. Like I just was on a really bad trip and now I'm coming down and have no idea how it will affect me, you know, in the long run. Like, has everything changed now?" She turned to Jocelyn, tears slipping down her cheeks. Karenza kept looking at her, the look full of beseeching. Jocelyn waited for the right words to come.

"You've been through a lot," she said. "You've been through a lot your whole life. But your life is young. And maybe how it's been tonight will help you to realize that not everyone wants to take advantage. But no, I don't think everything has changed. Scars don't just magically vanish. There will be times when you still react from the same knee-jerk place. But maybe now you'll be able to decide if that's useful or not. Does that make sense?"

"Yes," Karenza nodded, relaxing back into the chair. "It's a relief actually to hear what you just said. Are you some kind of a therapist, or what?"

Jocelyn laughed, "No, but I've had a lot of it."

"What *do* you do?" Karenza asked.

"I'm an artist and I also teach art part-time, which, come to think of it, borders on therapy sometimes."

"Really?" Karenza said, leaning forward. "An artist. Wow. What do you paint?"

Jocelyn smiled. "I used to hate that question, nearly as much as being asked *why* I paint. As if there was a choice. For the last couple of years I've been working on a series of large canvases. But, I don't know. It's hard to describe what they're about."

"Oh, please try?"

"Well. OK. When I was a little girl I used to love to look at things from an odd angle. So, say I'd lie on my side and look at my bedroom curtains so the folds were hanging horizontally instead of vertically. It gave them a magical quality because it was like it created a different dimension. Probably sounds nuts!"

"No! Not at all. But how do you go about painting that," Karenza asked. "Do you paint lying down or what?"

Jocelyn nearly laughed but said, "I have an old Polaroid camera I carry around, so when I find something that 'speaks' to me, I take a photo of it. Then when I get back to my studio I spend time turning the picture sideways, rotating it until I see something else. I'm aiming for something abstract yet based in reality. Something that makes people feel they're looking at something familiar, and maybe makes them question why."

"Sounds interesting," Karenza said, "I'd love to see them."

"Well, if we ever get out of here, come down to our hotel before we leave and I'll show you some slides of my work. Or better yet, come and visit us in New York. My studio is on the same floor as our apartment."

"Really?" Karenza said.

"Yes, really," Charles said. "We'd love to have you, I mean we'd love to . . ."

Karenza laughed, "It's all right, I know what you meant."

Kenneth returned with the wood and a bag of frozen prawns.

"Here," he said, giving them to Charles, "Sorry, no fish fingers."

He put the logs down and placed a couple of pieces on the fire. Karenza started to get up from his chair, "No, no," he said. "Stay where you are." He plonked himself down on the mattress, back to the couch, knees drawn up. "It's a bit like being in camp down here, isn't it?" he said, as Sarah gave him a cup of tea and some biscuits. "So, what did I miss?"

"Art therapy," Tom said. "And you'd better watch out, that mattress seems to have healing properties."

"Maybe you should try it then," Karenza said.

"Bit too close to the fire for me," he said, managing to give her a grin.

"It's interesting, isn't it?" Charles said. "How reluctant we are to talk about money."

"Oh, you noticed," Tom said, smiling at him. "Why do you think that is?" he asked.

"I don't know," Charles said, "Lots of reasons, really. I guess it can be a cultural thing, right? Like, here in England, it's considered rude to talk about money. I remember asking a friend of Jocelyn's how much it cost to rent her London flat and you'd have thought I'd asked her how often she masturbated. I guess there's a lot of shame attach to money, huh?"

"So what's your relationship to money?" Tom asked him.

"Hmmm. I'd say I have a pretty healthy attitude to money these days. I wouldn't mind having a bit more of it, I guess, but I think I've made some good investments that will build nicely over the next decade."

"Really?" Jocelyn exclaimed. "You're in the stock market?"

Charles looked at her and looked away. "*Yes*," he said. "Since before I met you."

"Ooh," Tom teased. "Do I detect another little secret?"

Once again, Jocelyn was piqued to discover that there were

things about Charles she didn't know. He knew everything about *her* finances. Why had he never told her about his "investments"— whatever they were. She shot such a look at him, he didn't need to hear what she was thinking. "Oh, come on Jocelyn," he said. "What's the big deal? I haven't lied to you. I just didn't think about it, really. You know, these bonds or whatever just tick over, I don't even think about it from one year to the next."

"Is that so? And just how much money is involved?"

"Well, it's hardly appropriate to discuss that here," he said, getting a bit uppity himself now.

"I thought you said it wasn't a big deal," she said. "So what's the problem?"

Actually, Charles didn't know why he hadn't told Jocelyn. He'd like to think it really wasn't a big deal, but after five years with a woman who insisted there was always a reason why one did or didn't do something, he knew there must be a reason for his withholding this particular piece of information. And there was that damn word again. Withholding. He hated to admit that's what he was doing. Not only about this stock market thing, but in general. What did he think he was gaining by not opening up completely? When had he become so mistrustful?

As if reading his mind, Jocelyn said, "You know, times like these, I really feel like you don't trust me. I feel like you assume every woman is like your ex-wife. I see the picture clearly now. If you don't marry me and don't disclose your finances then you think you won't run the risk of losing everything again. Well, you know what? Right now it's a close run thing. But then, maybe you don't consider me a valuable asset." She pulled away from him and walked over to the window, which stared back at her from its dark, unyielding surface. "What an idiot I've been," she said quietly, and before the tears had a chance to fall she turned and left the room.

46

. . . .

Instead of feeling her customary spiteful glee at witnessing her sister-in-law being humiliated, Sarah felt concern. The concern, for once, was not for herself, but primarily for Jocelyn, with whom during the course of this eternal night, she had felt the beginnings of a sisterly bond. But once again fear and confusion began its jig. Shouldn't she go to Jocelyn's rescue now, as Jocelyn had earlier come to hers? Did Jocelyn need rescuing? And if so, what on earth did Sarah have to offer in terms of comfort and advice?

"Well," Karenza said, tucking her feet underneath her as if to escape rising waters. "That's a bummer. I thought you two had it pretty together, but I guess that was just wishful thinking."

"Hey, wait a minute," Charles said, sitting up straighter on the couch, "This is not actually a life or death situation. I may have temporarily fucked up, but if you're entertaining the idea that there is any such thing as a perfect relationship then you are as mistaken as you are in believing all men are bastards."

"Well, to be honest I think you're a right dick. This is exactly the kind of thing between men and women that makes me crazy. Like you think, oh, this is my money and none of her business and anyway she's just a woman, she doesn't need to know these things."

"Karenza, please. Stop. Don't assume you know what I think. *I* don't even know what I think. Some things are a bit more complex than men are from Mars women are from Venus, okay?

Anyway, this has nothing to do with Jocelyn—or you for that matter—it's my shit."

"Yeah, well that's the trouble with relationships. People shit on each other."

"Look, there's a quantifiable difference between willfully hurting someone and hurting someone because you're a dumb ass."

"So, what are you going to do about it?" Karenza asked.

Charles fixed Karenza with a stern look, tucked the flashlight under his arm, rearranged the sling to keep the prawns in place and, hitching up his tartan skirt with the other hand, took a deep breath and headed for the door. "Wish me luck," he said, and left.

With Charles and Jocelyn gone, it felt as though four kids who didn't know each other had been left behind to fend for themselves.

Karenza looked at Sarah and Kenneth. They reminded her of so many couples she had served at the restaurant. Married couples who'd been together for ages yet sat in silence through three courses; not the awkward silence of strangers but the hostile silence of people who knew each other well and didn't like what they knew. To Karenza, Kenneth and Sarah seemed like two old people on a blind date.

As for Tom? She acknowledged, perhaps for the first time, that her behaviour might be confusing but she vacillated between feelings of anger at what she judged to be his ruthless superiority and something bordering on tenderness when she caught a glimpse of his frozen loneliness.

"Wow," she said, her voice like a shot in the dark, making the others jump. "Nothing like sex and money to fuck everything up is there?"

"Unavoidable, I'm afraid," Kenneth said. "Like death and taxes."

"Love and money just don't go together do they?" asked Sarah quizzically.

The other three looked at her, unsure if she had said something worth thinking about or something completely facile.

"Whatever," Karenza said. "I'm sure those two will decide to keep loving each other."

Charles made his way to the kitchen to get candles before looking for Jocelyn. Although he already had a torch, he knew how much she loved the ritual of lighting them. She said she liked the way it slowed her down, that it was almost like a meditation. Every evening she lit probably a dozen of them around the apartment and almost every night they bathed in candlelight, often sharing some of their most intimate conversations while soaking together in the tub. Although he was in a different kind of hot water now, he hoped that the lighting of a candle might soften the space between them.

Jocelyn had gone upstairs to the smallest of the three bedrooms; a monkish room with a single bed and an armchair. In front of the window was a small oak desk and chair and it was there that she sat in the dark and waited for the inky sea to become visible.

Although this was the most southwestern part of England, because of its land formation the coast here faced north, an oxymoron that had long fascinated Jocelyn, who'd first come here as a child. Looking to the east, she saw the faintest hint of dawn, not really a lightening of the sky so much as a small diminishment of the dark. The ivy framing the window trembled in a puff of wind, the wind mainly spent now. The rain, too, had stopped and to the west, stars were visible; a sprinkle of glitter holding on to the immutable fabric of night.

Although familiar with loneliness, Jocelyn hadn't felt this engulfed by it in a long time. It was as though, like a dormant virus, it had been reactivated just when she thought she was finally immune to it. Was it loneliness, or sadness? Was there a difference, or were they companions?

She knew this latest contretemps with Charles could be resolved if she waited for its initial energy to abate, but she also knew that it wouldn't be the last disappointment she'd experience if she stayed with him. It was this that fueled her sadness, the knowledge that no matter how much they loved each other, no matter how hard they worked at being honest, not only would they continue to disappoint each other from time to time, but that on the most basic level, in the core of her being, she, like everyone else, would always be alone. What was the point, she thought, why bother? If aloneness was an undeniable fact of existence then why not embrace it? Why not choose a solitary life, do as one pleased when one pleased; think uninterrupted thoughts, make decisions without consideration of the other, free oneself from vanity? Surely, to decide to go the rest of the way alone was to remove the terror of possibly being *left* alone, not to mention a way of avoiding grief?

No, it wasn't solitude that frightened her; it was the possibility that she couldn't count on Charles; because if he couldn't trust her, if he always had to withhold something in order to feel safe, then how could she trust him? Maybe there was no such thing as equality when it came to trust. Maybe trust and belief were foolish ideals destined to fall short; manmade absolutes, the existence of which humans demand in order to ward off the truth; that you can't count on anything; that there is no safety.

Poor Tom, she thought, there was a young man who obviously craved safety; safety from hurt, safety from loneliness, from vulnerability of any kind. Belief and trust certainly no longer existed for him. Yet still, he was human; he needed to be able to count on something, and he thought money was it. Poor fool. If only he could count on himself, she thought. But without the willingness to feel, could there be a self? Poor guy, how lonely he must be. And what had she done to be of help? She who professed to believe in love? How much love had she shown him? Who was she to judge others for withholding when she was so unwilling to give love to those most in need? Love, the thing she insisted was all encompassing, where did it go when scorned?

She jumped as the door opened. Charles stood there with a lit candle.

"Is it safe to come in?" he asked.

"Safer than not," she replied.

"Let's talk money then," Charles said.

It wasn't until they had fully accounted for themselves that they realized how freezing it was in the room, and although neither of them really wanted to be with others, neither did they want to be that cold.

"I'll tell you something money can't buy, besides love," he said.

"What's that?"

"Youth," he said. "Was a time, injury or no, frozen balls or not, I'd have your skinny arse on that skinny bed right now and make love to you until the sun came up."

"I'll definitely be taking you up on that," she said, and together they made their way downstairs.

"Oh, thank God," Karenza said, as Charles and Jocelyn made their re-entry.

"What did you think?" Charles said. "That there had been a murder in the pantry?" He walked over to her and without thinking kissed the top of her head, which to her surprise seemed completely natural, the way a father would do such a thing, coming home from work. She looked at Jocelyn, "So are you two sorted?" she asked.

"Better than ever," Jocelyn said, a big grin lighting her face.

"Really?" Tom said. "How's that?"

"We found out we're rich beyond compare," Jocelyn teased.

"Do share," Tom insisted.

"What d'you want to know?" she asked, and then seeing that she had put him on the spot, answered for him, "The secret to our success, right?"

"Something like that," he said.

"It's simple really. Communication. Whenever there's a gap in the communication, we're fucked."

"Hmm," Tom said. "Looked more to me like money was the problem."

"No," Charles said. "You're so wrong. Not *talking* about money was the problem."

"God, I'm cold," Jocelyn said.

"Here," Kenneth said, getting up off the mattress. "Your turn on the magic carpet."

"Me too," Charles said, hunkering down beside her.

Kenneth sat on the couch. "Sarah," he called, patting the space next to him, "come and keep me company."

Karenza, still curled up in what had been Kenneth's armchair, looked across at Tom. He, alone, was sitting in the same place he'd been in all night.

"So, Tom," Charles said. "Now Jocelyn knows we've got all this money, what should we do with it?"

Tom sat forward slightly in his chair, "You have a traditional portfolio, yes?"

"What does that mean?" Jocelyn asked.

"It means," Tom said, turning to her, "diversified investments in proven companies, otherwise known as blue chip. For instance," he said, turning back to Charles, "I'm guessing you have shares in DuPont, 3M, IBM, that sort of thing, right?"

"Right. How'd you know that?" Charles said. "Do you think that's unwise?"

"Not at all," Tom said. "It's as safe as investment can ever be. But if you're looking for high dividend yield you're going to have to turn to technology and start-ups."

What were they talking about, Sarah wondered. High-yield? Start-ups? And fancy Charles being in the stock market. She thought that was only for the wealthy. Of course, Charles was rather well off by her and Kenneth's standards. Not that he lorded it about. Still their visit to New York last year had certainly made it clear that Charles and Jocelyn's lifestyle was grander than hers and Kenneth's by a long chalk. They could fit the whole downstairs of their semi-detached into Charles and Jocelyn's living room, not to mention the size of the walk-in wardrobe. Of course, she'd known that American doctors were well-off, but she remembered thinking at the time that even with the addition of Jocelyn's salary they seemed to live in a carefree splendour that she found incomprehensible for a doctor and an art teacher. Was this what high yield meant? Was investment possible for people like her and Kenneth? Didn't you have to be rich to make money? And wasn't playing the market as they called it, just another description for gambling?

Oh, no, she couldn't bear it. She'd be constantly worrying about losing the precious little they had. She liked that Kenneth wasn't a risk taker. She didn't really know how much money they had, but she knew it was safely tucked away in a savings account. At least with a bank you knew where your money was, she thought, picturing a little drawer among rows of drawers all neatly labeled with their name and the names of their neighbors, all the drawers lined up like incubators in the vault of their branch of the Royal Bank of Scotland; a bank chosen by Kenneth because, as he said, when it came to money and bagpipes you couldn't beat the Scots. She reached for his hand.

The grandfather clock began to chime and the room went silent as each of them counted the strokes, time having taken on a different reality than the linear one they had all previously taken for granted. When the seventh chime ended, its reverberations seem to ripple out beyond the walls of the inn as if in an effort to catch up with the rest of time. Seven o'clock in the morning and yet, as each of them looked toward the window for a sign of dawn, it might as well have been seven at night, as if this night was eternal, as if time had done a bunk and left them all in limbo; each of them asking silent questions in an effort to convince themselves that time could be measured, had to be in order to keep one's place in it. How long had they been in this room? What time had they had dinner? When did the power go out? How long had it been since the last drink? When had Charles taken the last anti-inflammatory?

"What time does the sun rise here?" Jocelyn asked.

"About a quarter to eight," Karenza said.

Forty-five minutes, three quarters of an hour, what did it matter? It was a meaningless articulation of existence that man clung to in order to organize his survival. Jogging at six, breakfast at seven, school at eight, office by nine, laundry at ten, conference at eleven, dentist at noon, lunch at one, a lover at two, the hairdresser at three, groceries at four, a martini at five, the train at six, nursing home at seven, dinner at eight, homework by nine, a fight at ten, bed at eleven. And then what happened to time, when it wasn't playing tricks in dreams and nightmares?

"How exactly do you make your money?" Karenza asked the blunt question.

"You really want to know?" Tom replied.

"Yes, I really do," said Karenza.

"OK. Well, I advise investment banks about which Internet start-ups to invest in and then help them take those companies public," he said. It was the most engaged he'd been all night.

"And I assume you're good at that," she said.

"Yes, I am, actually." A boyish smile hovered at the corners of his mouth.

Karenza knew she had him now, knew that he finally felt safe enough to reveal something about himself. Perhaps this was the one area in his life where he felt confident and in control and, like a good courtroom lawyer, she knew that when the defendant felt infallible they were at their most vulnerable. And so she pursued her line of questioning not, as she would have done a few hours ago, because she wanted to nail him, but because she felt it was the last opportunity she might have to reach behind the well-kept façade.

"And what makes you so successful?" she asked.

"A combination of good instincts, professional skill and self-control," he said. She noticed, unlike so many times when he had spoken that night, his air of arrogance and cynicism had completely disappeared. "So, they must pay you a lot of money, these investment banks, yeah?"

"It depends," he said. "If they're taking a company public that I know will be successful then I take my fee in stock options. If I'm not wild about their choice then I take a direct fee. Either way it's a win–win situation."

There it was, she thought, the hubris of the gambler who believed he could beat the house. And of course he needed the hubris. He had to believe there was one area in life that was a win–win situation; he'd lost in all the others. She ran through them in her head: certainly he'd lost at love; God had long ago disappeared as an option. Equality was laughable. Civility, since Lily's "you know what . . . ?" was now the cruel mask of rejection, as for impermanence, well, of course everything and everyone came to an end, but until he came to an end he was going to be permanently wealthy.

"And how much money will be enough for you?" Karenza asked.

"Enough to be able to retire by the time I'm forty," he said, his confidence now a quiet presence in an almost gentle demeanor. He'd uncrossed his legs and one of them showed through the opening of his chenille skirt; a slim, hairless limb, like that of an adolescent boy.

"And exactly how much would that require," she asked.

"Five million liquid, five in assets and two fluid in the market," he said, his voice carrying a mixture of pride and tenderness as though he were a parent reciting the ages of his children.

"And what will you do with yourself when you retire?" she asked, feeling the moment had arrived to start shaking his boat. She saw his face tighten, just a hair, the foot of the exposed leg flexed, as if ready to give the boot to an annoying pup.

"That's a luxury I don't have time to think about at the moment, but in ten years I'll have all the time in the world," he said, his face relaxing into a grin.

"And what if you're wrong?" she asked.

"About what?" he said, crossing his legs and pulling the chenille back into place.

"About which companies will be a success. What if you make a mistake?"

"A mistake?" he said, a look of incredulity taking up the entire expanse of his face, the eyebrows raised above wide eyes, the cheekbones raw above a gaping mouth.

"I seriously doubt that happening," he said and she watched as he disappeared into derision, hubris's number one weapon of defence; when challenged in the area of certitude what was there to do but judge the accuser to be a fool.

"What a lonely place you live in," she said softly.

"And you don't?" he retorted, suddenly angry. "What do you think you have that I don't? Do you think your self-righteous activism will keep you good company for the rest of your life? You think you can count on love and loyalty; that marriage will save you from lonely nights or that a couple of kids are guaranteed to tend you in old age? Who in this room can tell me they're not really alone? Where is the happily married couple with the loving children? I *know* I'm alone. At least I have the courage to accept it and the wisdom to put my mouth where the money is. You're damn right I want my share of the pie and believe me, I have the recipe and the ingredients. . . ."

"And if the power goes out?" Jocelyn interrupted.

"Meaning what, exactly?" he said, anger and frustration throttling his voice.

"Meaning, if the power goes out how do you bake the pie?"

"If you're suggesting that the stock market is the oven then I rest my case. The stock market isn't the oven, it's the power and the power isn't going anywhere, it's increasing like it always has.

There maybe some brownouts along the way, but a loaf of bread will never sell for a shilling again. The market drives everything forward and now the Internet is driving the market. Either you get in the seat or you'll be driven off the road."

He got up, under the pretense of attending to the fire, but really he couldn't bear to see the way they were looking at him. He'd expected more argument. Instead, his words had left them stunned, but not, he saw, in awe and admiration, but in pity and sadness, a combination of human empathy and compassion that had arrived about fifteen years too late. Why he felt like crying he had no idea, but he certainly wasn't going to. He put a log on the fire, and then another. Took the poker and scattered the embers underneath them then put another log on top of the others, the embers reaching for the bark, sending out small flames that licked and darted, retreating and advancing as if searching for the ultimate space in which to gain purchase. Determined to make a blaze that would outlast the remains of the night, he piled on another log and the whole thing fell in on itself, the flames extinguished now as the wood morphed from potential fuel to instant damper. Tom watched in disbelief, shame burning through him; how could he have been so stupid.

"I hate to admit this," Kenneth said, kneeling next to Tom, "But I actually failed fire-making as a boy scout and I've been trying to earn that badge ever since." He held out his hand for the tongs. "Have I got a pyramid scheme for you," he said, and picking up the logs one at a time placed them upright in the grate, forming a sort of teepee and then, passing the last piece of paper to Tom, instructed him to crumple it and tuck it in behind the logs, then bending low he blew gently and steadily into the grate until the paper caught, pulling the heat of the embers with it until the fire roared back to life.

"Nice trick," Tom said, with genuine admiration.

"Oh, it's not a trick," Kenneth said. "It's a strategy," and reaching out his hand once more said, "How about helping this old dog up?" Tom grabbed his hand and placing his other under Kenneth's elbow, heaved him effortlessly to his feet. The two men looked at each other for a moment, still holding hands and then Kenneth patted Tom on the shoulder, "Thanks, son," he said and sat back down on the couch.

Jocelyn knew better than to say anything, but she longed to hug her brother, to tell him how good it was to see him coming back to life. She saw the connection between him and Tom, knew that Kenneth had felt it, too; two lonely, isolated men, one twice the age of the other, the trajectories of their lives stunted by a similar refusal to connect to their feelings. How fascinating it was, she thought, how differently people handle the same issues. Here was Tom, turning his pain into ambition and financial gain, while Kenneth had numbed his by toeing the line, obeying orders, settling for mediocrity. Different modes of control that both managed to keep emotion at bay. But she'd seen a crack in Kenneth's control a few times tonight and she hoped Tom had seen it, too; hoped that some small seed had been planted that might one day take root and blossom. The truth, she realized, was that she wanted to hug Tom, too, but sometimes love really did have to take a back seat and wait for the driver to let go of the wheel.

"Anyone want something to drink?" Karenza asked, getting up and going over to the sideboard.

Charles looked at his watch, nearly seven-thirty. If he and Jocelyn were at home, one of them would be putting the old Italian espresso pot on the stove and heating up some milk while the other popped around the corner to the little French pastry shop for croissants, a ritual that was too often interrupted if Charles was slated for early morning surgery. How wonderful it would be, he thought, to say goodbye to the dawn walk to the hospital, the pre-op scrub, the heart-pounding anxiety that preceded every incision, followed by the automatic shift to the mechanics of life and death; the sterile tray, the hum of anesthesia, the slap of the scalpel in the latexed palm; the blood and swabs and pus and malignancy of disease, side by side with his dis-ease; the awful weight of responsibility which no amount of reasoning could dispel and from which he could never be absolved by the relative awaiting the results of his performance. Surgery, like life, never offered the luxury of rehearsal. Although it was no game, still you either won or lost, and the score, out there in the hall, would never be settled; if you lost, everyone lost. How had he gone from being a young man eager to help others fulfill their lives, to a middle-aged surgeon trying to save lives full of cancer? Was it too late to return to plan A, to start every day with Jocelyn and coffee and croissants?

"We never talked about money, did we, Jocelyn? In our family, I mean. It was a taboo subject, wasn't it?" said Kenneth.

"No way," she replied. "Money and sex didn't exist in our house." There was a rather awkward silence as everyone recalled the event that brought about Jocelyn's conception, a silence which she interrupted with snort of laughter, "At least, money didn't."

"It was a class thing, really," Kenneth continued. "Cultural, too, I suppose. It just wasn't proper. And like so much else, one never questioned it." He paused again. "What a bloody repressive environment," he said, a note of anger evident in his tone. "When I think about it now, it's as though I was brainwashed before I even *had* a brain. It never occurred to me to ask about things. I mean it's just pathetic, isn't it? The English working class childhood of our era was basically experienced as a series of blanks filled in by silent but implicit messages, as though everyone believed that if you didn't actually mention anything then you didn't have to deal with it. Perhaps if I'd been a more imaginative child I'd have filled in the blanks with greater possibilities. As it was I understood that there wasn't a surplus of money in our family and it wasn't expected or encouraged that I be any different. So, I just decided to let the army take care of me. It seemed safe and sensible at the time," he said, looking ruefully at the fire. "But looking back, I see that fear ruled every decision I made. I may have been lacking imagination, but I was certainly able to come up with plenty of justification for my choices. Money was for the greedy people and greedy people could never have enough of it and they'd do anything to get it and I didn't want to be like that and, again because I lacked imagination and because I was afraid, I saw absolutely no option but to stick with what I had and be grateful for it. So I chose to compare myself with those who had less instead of with those who had more. I've never spent more than I have. Never had a credit card. Don't owe anybody anything. On the one hand it's quite a comfortable way to be. Quite civil, really," he said, smiling at Sarah. "We've done all right, haven't we?" She knew it wasn't really a question, and so she just patted his hand.

"Yes, sweetheart," she said, because really, what right did she have to say anything else?

"But surely," Tom said, "surely, there must have been times when you wished you had more money. There must have been something you wanted that only money could buy?"

Kenneth drained the last of his tea and looked in the cup as if more might magically appear. "Actually, I did at one point think it would be rather nice to have a little cottage in Brittany," he said.

"Did you?" Sarah asked. "You never told me that." The safety she had begun to feel since Kenneth had asked her to sit next to him already disintegrating, the precipice as threateningly near as ever.

"Well," Kenneth said, pursing his lips, "we couldn't afford it so . . ."

"But . . ." Sarah began to say and then on reflection decided to leave it.

As if finishing her thought, Tom said, "But you would have been able to afford it if your wife had worked, no?" He spoke as if Sarah wasn't even in the room and suddenly Kenneth had had it.

"You know what, Tom?" he said. "We must seem like such

easy prey to you, compared to all your wheeling and dealing and your clever bankers and all those bright young things. The sad thing is that it doesn't stop with money, does it? Not for people like you. I mean, what did you have to gain here tonight? It wasn't necessary to destroy us in order to expand your portfolio, was it? But you see, here's the thing about believing in money; in order to maintain the belief you have to destroy all other beliefs. And you still don't get it do you, Tom? We're all afraid and we all think believing in something will keep us safe from the thing we fear. So maybe I didn't want Sarah to earn money because I needed to feel like a man. I know. You look at me and see a pathetic old man. Believe me, I see that man in the mirror every bloody day. But guess what I have that you don't? I have a wife. I don't need more money, you idiot. I need more love." He put his arm around Sarah, "This is my nest egg and my retirement plan. Where's yours?"

Although Karenza had glanced at Tom a few times she, like the others, had been riveted by Kenneth's frontal attack. Only when he asked that final question did everyone look to Tom. Everyone except Sarah, who was transfixed by this man she'd been living with for more than thirty years during which time the closest to anger that she had seen him come was the occasional criticism of her drinking, muttered through clenched teeth as he made his way either to the garden shed, or bed.

Tom kept his eyes lowered as he attempted an apology.

"I'm sorry if I have offended you," he said. "I was just trying to defend my belief. And I suppose the inescapable reality of money and the role it plays in everyone's lives. Really, I have no interest in upsetting anyone."

"Apology accepted," Kenneth said. "But maybe you should be re-examining the role it plays in your own life. You can't get a cuddle from money."

"You can't get an orgasm from it, either," Karenza said, letting loose a wonderful cackle.

Sarah, whose eyes still hadn't left Kenneth's face, suddenly became distracted by something over his shoulder.

"Oh, look," she cried, pointing out the window where a faint glow could be seen just past Godrevy Island, the horizon once again a distant possibility. Dawn, that ephemeral moment of twilight before sunrise. The eve of day, one might say, which, like all eves, whether it was a new year or a wedding, a birth or just another Monday, brought with it excitement and trepidation, hope and regret; the desire to be propelled forward with new energy and new resolve tugged at by the longing to hold back, to retreat, to procrastinate, to redo, remake or rescind.

"Oh, thank God," Jocelyn said.

"Not him again," Sarah said and laughed along with the others.

"Hey," Karenza said. "We've got about ten minutes before sunrise. Why don't we get ourselves together and go outside to watch it?"

Ah, sweet youth, thought Charles, already reaching for his trousers hanging from the mantlepiece, and which were now dry, if stiff with mud. The three men then struggled much like middle-aged matrons on the beach, to get their pants on undercover of their skirts.

"Oh?" Jocelyn said, "My boots are still outside somewhere." Karenza offered her waitressing Doc Martens and went off to get them, while Tom went up to his room to get his jacket and change from his loafers into his leather boots. When they all met up in reception, Sarah sidled over to the girls. "Can you help me get rid of something?" she whispered, nodding towards the bar room.

"You guys go ahead, "Karenza said. "We'll be there in a mo. Oh and the best place to see the sunrise is right there," she said pointing out the window to a clearing between the trees. They were halfway down the hall when Karenza, gasped, "Oh, no!"

"What?" Jocelyn asked.

"The power line," Karenza said, already running back. She caught the men just as they were heading out the front door and reminded them about the line being down.

"Stay on the asphalt driveway and walk toward the bridge. We'll get a clear view from there," she said, and rejoined the women.

Like the magi, they made their way first to the bar room and then reverently through the kitchen. Jocelyn opened the back door and they stood there for a moment feeling the cool, still air. A blackbird called from a nearby tree. Down the lane a rooster crowed. The sea, no longer empowered by the raging wind lapped quietly at the foot of the cliff, its tone as hushed as a lullaby.

"We made it," Karenza said and, as Jocelyn had known she would, led them to the spot at the edge of the cliff where she had, so recently, nearly not made it. "Only rubbish goes over here," she said.

"On the count of three," Jocelyn said.

"Hold on to me," Sarah said and they each wrapped an arm around her waist and watched as she flung the bowl out to sea, the weight of the bowl separating itself from its contents before crashing on the rocks below.

"That's what I call hurling the hurl," Jocelyn said, and the three of them held onto each other as they laughed into the void, the stars extinguishing themselves in random order in the chaos of the dawn.

"Come on," Karenza said, grabbing their hands. "Let's catch up with the boys."

As they rounded the back of the inn, Sarah was surprised by how small it seemed as opposed to when they had arrived for dinner. Then it had seemed quite stately and impressive and she realized that although they had, for the most part, been confined to one room of it, she had felt as though she had been ensconced in a castle.

"Hurry," Karenza said, breaking into a run and pulling the other two with her. Sarah, who couldn't remember the last time she had run, giggled as she felt her breasts bouncing beneath her overalls. What a picture they must make, she thought, three tomboys on their way to meet the local lads. She felt the air crisp on her cheeks and a bubble of joy rose in her. She glanced at the others; Karenza with her ginger curls flying out behind her, Jocelyn's profile, as heroic as a figurehead, beneath its auburn cap. She felt her own salt-and-pepper pageboy spraying out from her scalp and thought maybe she'd get it layered when she got home. Oof, but she could do with some exercise.

A pale rose was beginning to bleed into the sky, like watercolor on wet paper and Jocelyn thought of Rothko and the simplicity of his canvases which, at first, seemed as empty as the sky, but which, like the sea, made you stay and look until you felt all that was there below the surface. That's how she wanted to paint, she thought. God but it was good to be alive.

Karenza, feeling the effort Sarah was making, slowed down a little and heard the mad music of a thousand birds fluting from pines and oaks and wondered if their feathers were as frayed as the trees, many of which had lost limbs in the night; some branches hanging by fibrous threads while others lay strewn across the lane.

"There they are," she cried, as they rounded a bend. The men stood close together, their backs to the women, obviously transfixed by something. As the women drew near they heard the roar of the swollen creek, the lane awash, the railings of the bridge long gone.

Charles and Tom turned, Charles holding out his good arm for Jocelyn. Kenneth, undeterred, continued explaining, with military precision, the mechanics that would be necessary to make a temporary bridge. Tom was mesmerized by Karenza, who suddenly looked so very young and innocent, and before he could form a greeting, she cried, "There it is!" pointing down river to the sea where now, like the sliver of an eyelid, the sun rose bloody at the horizon.

Jocelyn had slid in between Charles and her brother who had pulled Sarah close to him. Brother and sister made room for Karenza, linking arms with her, while Charles, his eyes never leaving the sunrise, reached for Tom with his arm, laying his wounded hand gently on Tom's shoulder. Six feet from them the river rushed on, a torrent of energy destined to return to its master, the air above it a juxtaposition of stillness, yet reverberating with sound. Down below, the village appeared, first in a soft focus of greys and blacks punctured here and there by lights, gradually defining itself in stone and street and spire as the sun rose, now a half circle spreading its light.

They stood in silence and watched as the sun became whole, it's color fading, its brilliance increasing as it sailed higher, their faces luminous.

"There's something worth believing in," Jocelyn said, and as one they turned and started back to the inn.

If it weren't for the arboreal debris, it would have been hard to believe that a storm had raged through the night. Yet the stillness was almost eerie, carrying a kind of suspense with it, as if perhaps all was not well, but merely the calm before another storm. No one spoke, each of them feeling not so much at a loss for something to say, as hesitant to sully the atmosphere. It was as though, Jocelyn thought, they had all been cut down to size now that they were out in the world. All the facts and fictions of their lives, their hurts and longings, regrets and hopes, all the blame and recrimination, projections and plans, the revelations and beliefs, all of which had been irritated, compressed and purged by their confinement seemed, now that they had been released into a new day, not exactly trivial, but diminished. They had, she thought, come to know each other through duress and disaster, as if the storm itself had insisted they match its destructive power by willing them beyond themselves, stripping them of their stories, as if to do so would guarantee annihilation. Yet here they were, godless but equal, a little shy, but grateful. Even Tom felt a tentative sense of belonging.

It was light now, and the light was as crisp as the air. A bush of holly twinkled like Christmas, its berries bright with cheer and the trunks and branches of every tree and shrub glistened as the sun lit their rain-soaked apparel.

"Oh, listen," Kenneth said, suddenly stopping and holding up a hand. The trees were a-chatter with birds, all of them indistinguishable except to Kenneth, who was now cocking his head like a robin. "There," he said, pointing to a stand of oaks on their left. And they listened as a series of seven notes separated themselves from the chorus; a pause, and then, as if to embellish the fact of its existence, the same clear-throated voice issued nine notes. There was nothing particularly musical about it, no great operatic trill; it was its matter-of-factness that made it clearly audible.

"A chiffchaff," Kenneth informed them. "They love oaks and they like to winter here."

"Unlike the riff-raff we get in summer," Karenza said, the ensuing laughter drowning out the entire avian choir.

"I didn't know you were a birder," Jocelyn said.

"Well, I'm not, you know, avid. But this area is full of treats. There's the lapwing, and the fire-crest, which has a piercing whistle. Then you have the snipe with its squeaky wheel. Oh, and yesterday I saw a black-tailed godwit."

"That was me, dear," Sarah said, and even Tom had a good laugh.

"Sounds like the beginning of a new game," Charles said. "What would I be, Kenneth?"

"Oh, you'd make a good stonechat and my sister is most definitely the fire-crest."

"Well, please don't call me a snipe," Karenza pleaded.

"Maybe you'd like to be a snow-bunting. They're somewhat rare here, but they have a very sweet song."

"What about me?" Tom asked, sounding like a young boy not wanting to be left out.

"I'd wager you're a razorbill. It's a sea bird, comes here to winter and to breed."

Tom thought for a while and then asked, "And what about you?"

"Oh, I think I'll opt for the heron," Kenneth said, and slowly lifted one leg, bent at the knee, jerked his head forward, and flapping his arms leaped into the air.

They rounded the bend and the inn came suddenly into view with a blast of radiant colour, its ivy-covered exterior lit a glamorous red by the sun.

"Wow," Charles exclaimed. "Who knew that's where we were all night."

"Was it always called The Morvah?" Jocelyn asked.

"Originally," Karenza said, "it was called Chy Morvah which is old Cornish for sea-house. The Morvah is supposed to be more upmarket but actually means sea-grave!"

"Oh, that's unfortunate," Jocelyn said. "Thank goodness it didn't live up to its name last night."

"Let's go back in before the rescue squad arrives," Charles suggested, picking up the pace.

"What about your name, Karenza," Tom asked, "I've never heard it before; is it Cornish, too?"

"Yes," she said, turning to him, "It means 'love,' can you believe it?"

He grabbed his chest and groaned in mock horror and acting as if he had received a direct hit, staggered backwards off the driveway onto the wet grass his feet connecting with voltage from the downed line, his body arcing backwards as he flew, the sky so clear, so blue, his heart swelling; he saw Karenza start to run towards him, saw Charles hold her back and wondered why love couldn't rescue him and he wondered why if love was so unreachable it still had the power to touch his heart; he wondered what the razorbill sounded like and longed to hear its song; the sea roared in his ears, his mother called his name, he wondered if his father would be home for tea, he heard his name again and wondered if he was the piper's son and wondered if the piper had come a calling, wondered why he was flying backwards and wondered if it was too late to change direction, wondered if the others would wait for him and filled with wonder he began his descent, heard the church bells and then the grandfather clock chiming eight and he wondered if there was still time ...?

ACKNOWLEDGEMENTS

Of all the pages that make up this book, none are more challenging to write than these. Partly because it signals the very end of a long journey, but also because, unlike the other pages, these have no possibility of being adequately expressed.

To Jon Smith, for introducing me to copy editor Barbara Richard. Thanks, Jon. You were the first to push the boat out. To Barbara Richard, who not only is fantastic at what she does but does it without fanfare, with great respect, and comes in on time and on budget. To Gianni and Luana, thank you for coming down the hill every evening during the months I was writing the first draft and insisting I recount, in Italian, the latest events at The Morvah. My deepest thanks to my editor, Sarah Westcott, for helping me assassinate prideful passages and for metaphorically and literally holding my hand. To my early readers for their time and their honesty: Sharon and Paul Mrozinski, thank you for "getting'" me and for picking me up each time I fell. Vivian Ubell, thank you for thirty-five years of believing in me. David Sumberg . . . thanks for the entropy! Helen Whitney, thank you. To be validated by you is an honor. Jody and Larry Carlson, my thanks for your kind words and generous hearts. My thanks to John Ryan, Melissa, Jim and Patrick O'Shaunessy for invaluable help in getting the "money" part of this story to ring true. Joshua Kercher Jara, thank you for reading so deeply in a language not your native tongue. Your insight and compassion belie your years. To Bert Shaw, your help accompanies me every day.

I first had the idea for this book in 2001, wrote two chapters and put it away for the next twelve years. In 2013 it called to me again and the first draft flew out of me and onto the page in five thrilling months. During the hard months of trying to get this book between covers, I was fortunate to have the encouragement of Julie Burstein and my son-in-law David Weller, both of whom tried valiantly to help me "brand" myself in order to gain a bigger readership before publication. Your suggestions and support were crucial to helping me realize and accept that "branding" ain't for me. I'm an old-fashioned girl, it turns out.

The decision to self-publish set me free. It also brought its own challenges. Enter Barbara Richard, again. Dear Barbara, thank you for being the best bookends I've ever had! And thank you for giving me Claudia Martinez, whose skills as text designer and typesetter are coupled with kindness and encouragement. These two women, when I was at my moment of deepest despair, said the magic words, "Leave it to us, we'll take care of it."

And then there is Joel Meyerowitz, my husband, friend, cheering squad and shoulder to cry on. My dear Joel, from my heart and on my knees, thank you: for listening to everything I've written during the last twenty-five years, for your encouragement and belief, and for showing me by example that the best reward is in the doing.

And to you dear reader, thank you for taking the time to enter these pages. I hope it was a good experience for you and that it maybe even sheds a little light on your own beliefs. If you would like to stay in touch, I would be honoured. You can do so by following me at www.feelingourwayaround.com.

ABOUT THE AUTHOR

Originally from England, Maggie Barrett is a writer and artist currently living on a farm in Tuscany with her husband, the photographer Joel Meyerowitz. The author of four novels, a collection of short stories, and the play *Give It Up*, which she performed Off Broadway, Maggie is currently working on a collection of essays. You can follow her adventures at www.feelingourwayaround.com.

Lightning Source UK Ltd.
Milton Keynes UK
UKHW010401230822
407680UK00008B/196/J